FINANCING

YOUR CONDO, CO-OP, OR TOWNHOUSE

David Reed

American Management Association

New York • Atlanta • Brussels • Chicago • Mexico City • San Francisco
Shanghai • Tokyo • Toronto • Washington, D.C.

Special discounts on bulk quantities of AMACOM books are available to corporations, professional associations, and other organizations. For details, contact Special Sales Department, AMACOM, a division of American Management Association, 1601 Broadway, New York, NY 10019.
Tel: 800-250-5308 Fax: 518-891-2372
E-mail: specialsls@amanet.org
Website: www.amacombooks.org/go/specialsales
To view all AMACOM titles go to: www.amacombooks.org

This publication is designed to provide accurate and authoritative information in regard to the subject matter covered. It is sold with the understanding that the publisher is not engaged in rendering legal, accounting, or other professional service. If legal advice or other expert assistance is required, the services of a competent professional person should be sought.

Library of Congress Cataloging-in-Publication Data

Reed, David (Carl David), 1957-
  Financing your condo, co-op, or townhouse / David Reed.
      p. cm.
  Includes index.
  ISBN-13: 978-0-8144-8062-5 (pbk.)
  ISBN-10: 0-8144-8062-4 (pbk.)

  1. House buying—United States. 2. Condominiums—United States. 3. Apartment houses, Cooperative—United States. 4. Row houses—United States. I. Title.
  HD259.R434 2009
  332.7'22—dc22

                                                              2009004051

Printing number

10 9 8 7 6 5 4 3 2 1

Contents

Preface

I'VE BEEN IN THE MORTGAGE INDUSTRY FOR 20 YEARS, first as a mortgage broker in San Diego, California, before moving to Texas to become a mortgage banker, where I still work today. When I first started in the mortgage business, there were but a few loan choices available, all offered by a relatively small number of lenders.

I write this book from experience, and I give it to you straight. I can't count the times I've read articles or columns from real estate finance "experts" who have never been in the mortgage industry much less placed a mortgage loan for someone.

I have placed home loans and still do. I also have more articles, books, and columns on the topic of real estate finance than any other author in the country. Heck, probably all over the world.

I enjoy writing, but I enjoy more how to explain sometimes complicated topics into "bite-size" chunks that are easily understandable, without the industry jargon. Sometimes I think that real estate loan programs are made to be confusing.

Condominiums, cooperatives, and townhouses are a bit of a different breed when it comes to financing. Unfortunately, information on exploring the various financing arrangements for these properties is typically buried in a footnote in some mortgage book somewhere.

Financing these types of properties takes a bit more research than your bread-and-butter conventional mortgage loan made for a three-bedroom, two-bath brick home out in the suburbs. There are so many more conditions that need to be addressed from a financial perspective that simply don't apply to a traditional house.

In the late 1990s, mortgage banking grew in terms of both loan volume as well as the types of new mortgage loans being invented. When one mortgage company came up with a different type of mortgage product, soon thereafter everyone had to offer the same mortgage loan.

Loans became more complicated, with terms used nowhere else. In fact, many loans became so complicated that even the loan officers marketing those loan programs didn't understand the loan terms themselves.

Did you know that if your prospective condo rents out some of its units to vacationers, it is nearly impossible to get financing? Did you know that your condominium, townhouse, or cooperative arrangement has to be approved prior to obtaining financing? Did you know that your lender will question the management companies of these projects and ask things such as, "How many of these units are owner occupied?" and "Does the project have enough insurance to cover repairs and maintenance?" or "Are any of these units rented out and, if so, how many?"

If your potential purchase doesn't meet the lenders' guidelines, then you'll pay a higher interest rate, perhaps put more money down, or not get financing at all.

This book covers all aspects of mortgage lending, from how to save on closing costs to finding the best lender to refinancing your loan. You don't need to buy multiple books to get all of your condo, townhouse, or co-op questions answered. You can get them all answered right here in this book, and after reading *Financing Your Condo, Co-op, or Townhouse*, you'll be armed to the teeth with consumer information found nowhere else to help you get the best financing package available in the marketplace today.

CHAPTER 1

Condos, Co-ops, and Townhouses: How Are They Different and How Are They Similar?

SO YOU WANT TO OWN A CONDO, EH? Live the urban lifestyle, park the car, and walk to work. You know, all the "condo" things. Condominiums first began to take hold in the real estate marketplace in the late 1970s, offering an alternative to the often more expensive single-family residence.

Or is a "cooperative" or "co-op" in your plans? Co-ops, found in most major (primarily East Coast) cities, offer a similar alternative to apartment or single-family homes. Although co-ops are similar to condos, they're not the same as condos.

Townhouses, too, are just a tad different from traditional single-family residences. They also are grouped into a legal "community" that has certain rules similar to condominium or co-op arrangements (we'll discuss those rules in detail in chapter 5) yet appear more like a traditional single-family structure.

Either way you decide, condos, co-ops, and townhouses represent different lifestyles and offerings from living in a suburban or rural home.

But first, exactly what is a condo, a co-op, or a townhouse? Technically, a condo is a legal association in which the individual owns the interior of his or her own unit and the entire group equally shares ownership in the common areas of the complex.

This condominium association is charged with enforcing the rules and regulations set forth in the condominium's legal documents called *Covenants, Conditions and Restrictions*, or CC&Rs, which we'll examine in more detail in chapter 5.

When you first imagine a condo, you might think of a tall, downtown building encasing lots of individual living spaces. And in many instances that would be correct. But a condo doesn't have to be all in one building, or be tall or short. A condo may consist of separate buildings, some connected, some not. A condo can be a collection of single-family residences that from the outside don't look like a typical condominium at all. In other words, you can't recognize a condo just by looking at it.

CONDOS

There are different types of condos, and some of the differences can affect the type of financing you obtain. There are:

> High-rise, mid-rise, and low-rise

> One- to two-unit condos
> Condominium conversions
> Condotels

High-Rise, Mid-Rise, and Low-Rise

These terms refer to how many stories, or floors, there are in the project. A low-rise is typically one to three stories high, a mid-rise is four to nine stories, and any condo more than nine stories is a high-rise. Typically, high- and medium-rise condominiums are found in downtown, urban areas.

Sometimes lenders will require a bigger *down payment* for a high-rise condo than for a low- or mid-rise. Financing a high-rise could result in a higher *interest rate* or an additional lender fee as well.

One- to Two-Unit Condos

Sound a bit odd? Why would anyone have a one- or two-unit condo? What's the point? In fact, this trend began when people figured out they could buy a stand-alone duplex (two attached houses) or a fourplex—four separate houses—all connected.

The idea caught on when turning a duplex into a two-unit condo made sense. The owner could buy the duplex, turn it into condos, and sell those condos separately instead of selling the duplex all at once. The same goes for a triplex or for a fourplex. A buyer acquires a multiunit structure, does all the legal work to turn it into condos, then sells them one by one, which often results in more profit for the *seller*. However, there is little demand in today's real estate market for one- or two-unit condos compared to single-unit, owner-occupied real estate.

Condominium Conversions

A conversion is typically an apartment building that has been turned into condominiums. Lenders may have special condo-conversion guidelines that the developer must meet. For example, making sure the condos have separate firewalls or stipulating that other recent conversions in the area must be 80 percent presold (which means that if there are 100 units, 80 of them must already have *sales contracts* on them).

You can't recognize a condominium conversion just by looking at it. Nor can you tell whether your lender will put any special conditions on it. But a little advance research will tell you.

Condotels

One can probably guess what a condotel is: a condominium complex where individuals own the condos, but some or most are rented out by the day, week, or month, just like a hotel.

In this case, you can tell a condotel when you see it because it will have a check-in desk and hotel-like amenities. Few lenders make loans on condotels.

Common Areas

Condominiums have common areas such as sidewalks, swimming pools, recreation rooms, and health clubs. These common areas belong to the condo owners. No, you may not remove "your section" of the sidewalk and haul it upstairs. You may not claim a stake in your 1/100 of the pool and make the other swimmers keep out. Everyone owns the structure and amenities equally, as well as the land where the structures stand.

CO-OPS

A cooperative, or co-op, is similar to a condominium arrangement. In fact, if you were to look at two high-rise buildings standing next to each other, you could not tell the condo from the co-op (unless there's a sign out front). The difference is, instead of buying a particular unit in a co-op, you are buying a share of ownership in the entire cooperative. It's like a corporation where you own shares of stock; the association owns the complex and the individual owners buy their shares. Lenders sometimes call this "share financing" because the *loan* you get isn't to purchase the property itself but instead your share of the cooperative. The cooperative will also have its own association (like a Board of Directors) that makes sure the cooperative's rules and regulations are enforced. Co-ops are typically found in densely populated metropolitan areas. There are numerous in New York City and Washington, D.C., but they're not too popular throughout the rest of the country.

Co-ops are similar to condos, with a couple of distinctions: Co-ops have one big *mortgage* for the entire complex—if there is financing on the building at all. Then, individual buyers of the cooperative shares essentially earn the right to lease from the cooperative. When you make an offer for a "share" in a cooperative, you will not only apply for a loan to purchase that share but also apply to the board of directors. The board will review your financials and poke around in other aspects of your life to make sure they want you as a neighbor. You can't be discriminated against because of race, sex, age, or other prohibited discriminatory factors. You can, however, be turned down by the board if your financials aren't up to their standards, if you've had recent credit problems, or even if your lifestyle is an issue. If the cooperative is made up mostly of retirees who want a nice, quiet life, and a notorious rock star wants to move in, the Board may not approve the purchase due to the potential of all-night parties and loud music. On the other hand, when you make an offer on a condo, you need only be concerned with getting financing.

TOWNHOUSES

Again, townhouses are much like condos. Typically, they are described as separate structures sharing similar outside walls. But different from a condo, a townhouse allows you to own the land it sits on as well—a small difference, but a difference nonetheless. Similar to a condo, you need only be concerned with getting a mortgage on a townhouse. You don't have to apply to a board of directors. Townhouse financing is identical to condominium financing. And like condos, townhouses have governing associations.

Townhouses often resemble duplexes—two houses sharing a common, separating wall, with separate utility meters.

Condos, co-ops, and townhouses share similar underwriting guidelines that are distinct from single-family structures, duplexes, triplexes, or fourplexes. We'll address the financing options in detail in chapter 3.

A lender may require a condo, co-op, or townhouse to have a majority of its units occupied by their owners. A house wouldn't have that requirement; it wouldn't make sense. A house either is or is not occupied by the owner. If it's not, the lender can ask for more down payment and charge a higher interest rate. With a condo, co-op, or townhouse, if the lender requires that the majority of the owners live in the units and it turns out that they do not, the lender might not make the loan at all.

Or compare a traditional duplex with a duplex that has been converted to a condo. A lender may ask the duplex buyer to put at least 10 percent down to get financing. But if the duplex were a condo and there were two units, neither of which was occupied by one of the owners, a lender again might not issue a mortgage—or may require a much bigger down payment.

Lenders don't really have "special" loan programs just for condos, co-ops, and townhouses. You'll still find a 30-year *fixed-rate mortgage* or an *adjustable-rate mortgage* for these types of properties. But they do have special requirements for those associations that must pass muster before that 30-year fixed rate can be had.

Although these three property types are similar to one another, they must be distinguished from a single-family residence when it comes to financing. There are guidelines that must be followed, down payment requirements can vary, and credit requirements can be different.

Because the three property types are similar to one another, throughout this book instead of saying "condo, co-op, or townhouse" each time, I'll simply use the term "unit" or "property" when the information can apply to all three. Condos and townhouses are identical in every instance when it comes to financing, yet there are some differences between them and co-ops. When those differences arise, I'll address them specifically.

Knowing how the financial aspect of ownership works is critical before you go shopping. You may find a high-rise condo downtown that's more than 12 stories and want to put zero down. Good luck with that. Or perhaps you're looking at a nice unit near a college campus that rents out to lots of students. Guess what? You could find yourself paying a higher interest rate. Unless you structure your financing the way it's supposed to be structured, you may not even get financing at all.

Financing a single-family residence is simple compared to a condo, townhouse, or co-op. A house needs a qualified buyer, and the property itself must meet a minimum appraised value. That's it. You can move in. But with any of these three property types, not only will the buyer and the property need approval, but the entire *project* must be reviewed and approved as well. We'll discuss those rules in chapter 5. They include things such as knowing whether or not one entity owns 10 percent or more of the units in the project, whether there is enough money in the Homeowners Association (HOA) budget to cover emergency repairs, or even if the owners of the individual units are behind in their monthly HOA dues.

Financing a house has none of that. And although financing a condo, co-op, or townhouse isn't as daunting as it sounds, these differences are critically important.

This book will give you everything you need to know to finance the condo, co-op, or townhouse that is perfect for you.

THE LIFESTYLE

These properties offer a different lifestyle from a stand-alone home. They cater to specific desires. There are no lawns to mow. Okay, there may be lawns, but individual owners don't do the mowing. Or water the flowers. Or sweep the driveway. Get the picture? There's simply less maintenance.

Does the roof leak? If you owned a home you'd be calling a roofing repair company and shelling out a few thousand bucks for a new roof. But if the roof leaks at one of these other property types, the cost will be divided up among the individual owners or paid via a condominium or townhouse association's insurance policy.

If you're in an urban setting, you may not own a car because you live close to where you work. You can walk to work or take mass transit or a taxi. Retail shops abound. Grocery stores and coffee shops offer pretty much anything you could want. If there is a 900-unit condo springing up downtown, you can bet there are plenty of retailers waiting to set up shop and provide their services nearby. Such convenience makes these properties attractive to certain buyers.

Condos, co-ops, and townhouses appeal to some buyers

and turn other buyers off. Some folks simply may not like the lifestyle. I'm not interested in such properties because I like my lawn and my trees. I enjoy mowing and taking care of our landscape. It's all about personal preferences. A single-family home has no intrinsic advantages over a condo, co-op, or townhouse. It's the same with automobiles: Different kinds of cars appeal to different kinds of people.

And, as with automobiles, different models come with different price tags. One potential advantage of these types of properties over single-family homes is price. In fact, these units typically sell for less than their stand-alone counterparts. You can find lots of one- or two-bedroom condos at entry-level prices. There is no standard "savings per square foot compared to a house" formula that you can apply everywhere, but many condos have an entry-level appeal that single-family structures do not. How can they do that?

When a builder builds a condo project, he has a predetermined amount of square footage he can work with—and he wants to make as much money as he can. So far, so good. Now, based on the market, he may decide to include more one-bedroom units and fewer three-bedroom units. The square footage is the same; the builder just moves some walls around to create some new condos.

Now, you won't find too many one-bedroom homes. Few people would consider buying one. But you will find one-bedroom condominiums. After living in one for a few years, the owner may want to move into a house or a larger condo. If so, she'll sell her unit for a profit and move up to a bigger place.

Lower prices also mean greater affordability; it doesn't take as much monthly income to qualify for a loan if the selling price is lower than comparable houses in the area.

Another neat feature: These types of properties offer many amenities that may be cost-prohibitive for a single house. Want a swimming pool? Your townhouse has one. But with a house, you must put in your own.

Workout gym? Many projects have health clubs onsite, saving you money on gym memberships and keeping you healthy (if you actually work out, of course). It's there if you want it.

Many properties have security gates and security guards—surveillance cameras and such. Once inside your unit, you should feel safe.

Different amenities, access to work and play, and pride of ownership all come with owning a condo, co-op, or townhouse.

So everything is good, and there is no downside—right? Again, it depends on your point of view. You will suddenly have lots of neighbors. If they are loud, it could be a problem. Someone could be having a party right below your unit; you weren't invited and the music is loud. Boom! Boom! Boom!

Yes, management can calm them down and you can file a complaint, but it's an annoyance.

You'll belong to an HOA. Some HOAs are better than others. The not-so-good ones are often made up of neighbors acting like the Noise Police, filing complaints over the tiniest little thing. You left your shoes out on the sidewalk last night and you're not supposed to. Do that again, and you'll face a fine!

THE HOA

The HOA is a legal entity made up of condo or townhouse unit owners. It makes sure that the rules are followed; it listens to owners and addresses the complex's physical areas and legal functions. Cooperatives have similar arrangements; their boards perform the same functions as an HOA.

Do you want to join the HOA? Actually you have no choice. Part of owning a condo or townhouse is joining the HOA and paying your monthly HOA dues.

These monthly HOA dues can cover various expenses, such as insurance for the property and various business costs. Yes, you must pay an HOA fee, but because the HOA covers the complex's insurance, you won't have to take out a separate insurance policy like a homeowner would.

The HOA forms a board made up of condo owners that enforces the condo rules, listens to its owners, and keeps up the property. But its primary goal is to make sure all the owners follow the established rules, the CC&Rs. That's really just lawyer language for "follow all the rules."

Co-ops have similar rules and regulations their shareholders must follow as well.

Common CC&Rs include conforming to certain color schemes when painting the exterior of your unit or using a particular type of window covering or awning. You might not be able to fly a flag on a pole attached to your front door.

No two stand-alone houses are exactly alike. Many have

similar floor plans and were built by the same builder, but he may have added a few square feet here or an awning or different roof there. If you're trying to determine value, houses aren't as easy to assess as units that are right next to one another or in the same condo complex. We'll discuss this aspect of value in more detail in chapter 3.

Yet these property types are very similar. Their floor plans are typically the same for several—if not all—of the other one- or two-bedroom units. This means that if one property owner doesn't follow the CC&Rs and lets his or her unit fall behind in repairs, keeps an unsightly appearance, or engages in other value-deflating practices, the other units may lose their value as well.

Rarely will two properties right next to each other sell for different prices at around the same time. They're easy to value because of their sameness. If someone keeps his or her condo in poor shape, inside and out, a prospective buyer would offer less for that condo compared to other condos—and that sale is recorded publicly. Then, the next time someone thinks about selling his or her property, the real estate agent will research sales in that complex and see that it's worth, say, $200,000 based on past sales. There's nothing in that information that said it sold for less than it should have because the owner didn't take care of it.

All HOAs have CC&Rs designed not to make the place feel like a jail, but to maintain the grounds and general upkeep, and to make sure the units maintain their value by preventing owners from allowing them to fall into disrepair.

Lenders can review the CC&Rs when deciding whether to place a loan on a property. Sometimes these regulations are too onerous and a lender won't place the loan. Such instances are few and far between, especially today. But they still happen from time to time. CC&Rs can have language stating that the HOA must approve the buyer moving in. Or they may have what is called a "first right of refusal," which means that if an owner wants to sell his or her unit and move away, he or she must let the HOA have the first shot at buying the unit instead of putting it on the open market.

In either instance, this could appear to be discriminatory (an association reviewing potential buyers or buying a unit from a seller and proceeding to pick and choose among potential buyers). When lenders see this type of language, they often will make the HOA revise it before they will issue a loan.

Though such activity is rare, it does occur at times, so you need to be aware of it. How do you know what the HOA rules are? Will you find out only after your loan is approved with the condition that the CC&Rs must be reviewed?

You can ask for a copy of these CC&Rs up front and review them for yourself. Boards are made up of people. Sometimes people can be, well, people. They can mess things up through overzealous application of rules and ruin the fun for everybody. But as long as you don't try and plant your native totem pole outside your front door or paint your roof pink, you'll probably be fine. But there are some things to look out for.

LAWSUITS, FEES, AND HOAs

When reviewing the CC&Rs you should look for a couple of items in particular. First, are there any pending lawsuits either on behalf of or against the HOA? Lenders will not issue any sort of mortgage on a condo, co-op, or townhouse if there is current litigation. For a couple of reasons.

One, if the association loses a lawsuit the owners may be asked to pony up some additional funds to help pay for either the lawyers involved or the settlement. If so, find out how much.

Lenders need to know that, because a special assessment for an irregular payment could harm a borrower's ability to repay a debt. If a lender determines that your total monthly outlay for housing expenses should be no greater than $2,100 and suddenly the owners are hit with an additional fee, you might not qualify for a loan. This additional fee may be one big fee or it may be broken down into smaller amounts paid monthly. If the owners are asked to pay another $100 per month, then that limit of $2,100 would be exceeded by $100 and the lender may turn down the loan application.

It doesn't matter about the nature of the lawsuit. It could be as minor as a contractor using the wrong shade of paint on a fence post.

The CC&Rs say you must pay your HOA fees. You have no choice. Nor may you refuse to pay due to nonperformance or because of a dispute with a neighbor. You gotta pay. And if the

CC&Rs state that the HOA board can raise your fees whenever and however much they want, then you have no choice but to pay.

Most HOAs are sensitive to this. They certainly want owners and tenants to be good neighbors, so they won't assess the owners out of existence. If assessments are excessive, no one will buy the units.

What is excessive? Look at similar HOA fees for other projects in the area and start from there. Also, look at the history of the HOA. How many times in the past have HOA fees been raised? Are they raised often? Once per year? Once per five years? If you see a regular pattern of fee increases such as once or twice per year, do some more homework and find out why. It shouldn't be this way.

You also need to see if the association has a history of suing people or being sued. HOAs often include attorneys as board members. Such attorneys are likely to live in the complex. Sometimes you may find an overzealous attorney who is all too happy to file a suit (using her own law firm, of course). This may persuade a lender not to make a mortgage loan.

There are some simple guidelines to steer you away from bad properties. But first, don't assume that all properties are run by control freaks; they're not. And regardless of how you finance and acquire a condo, co-op, or townhouse, getting in with a group of surly neighbors will not make you happy.

CHAPTER 2

What to Look for in a Property and How to Find the One That's Right for You

OKAY, I ADMIT IT. That's a bold claim. The "right property" is a moving target. It may even be an unachievable goal because with nearly any property there is something that could be improved upon. Better view, nicer lighting, more amenities. But before we get into the financing aspects, let's look at a few ways to help find the best property for you. We'll look at the different types of properties and the differences between buying new from a developer or builder and buying from an individual.

First though, one of the most common questions people ask when first starting to look is, "Do I need to use a real estate agent to help me find the right property?"

USING A REALTOR

Heck yes. And why wouldn't you? Maybe you think that hiring and paying for a Realtor is expensive and unnecessary. But in reality, it's not you who compensate your Realtor when she works with you in finding a new condo. It's the seller of the property who pays your Realtor.

When a Realtor lists a property (which means putting it up for sale), the Realtor will also post how much she will pay another Realtor for bringing a buyer to the closing table. Typically, the split is 50/50 between the listing agent and the buying agent.

For instance, a condo is listed at $300,000 and the seller is willing to pay the listing agent 5 percent of the sales price to market and sell the home. That's $15,000. Now, the listing agent may split that fee 50/50, so the buyer's agent gets $7,500.

That means you don't pay an agent to help you—the seller does.

If a Realtor who works every single day in the real estate market knows the hot spots, knows the bargains, knows what holds value and can help you negotiate the sales price, then why wouldn't you use a Realtor? It's free!

Realtors can specialize in certain areas of the city. Or a Realtor may have a run of recent sales in a downtown market full of condos and can keep you from overpaying by suggesting a reasonable offer to make. Not only do you want a Realtor who specializes in certain geographic areas, you want one who specializes in the condos, co-ops, or townhouses within those areas. Don't bring a Realtor from the north side of town if you want to live on the south side.

A Realtor can also give you the inside scoop on a complex—things the general public may not know, such as how long a property was on the market before it sold, or whether the sellers are offering any additional incentives to buy (such as helping pay for *closing costs* or paying off an assessment). We'll discuss closing costs in more detail in chapter 6.

Now that you know what a Realtor can do for you, how do you find a good one? After all, not every Realtor can be the best on the block. Some don't work full time. Some are new to the business.

The first thing you should do is get referrals from friends and neighbors. You need someone who has been in the industry for several years; they're the ones with the best contacts. You need someone who's serious about the business and has a good history of working with buyers.

You also want to work with a Realtor you feel comfortable with—one you can relate to. I have associations with different Realtors to whom I refer buyers. But I don't make referrals randomly; it's not just a simple rotation through my Rolodex. For example, I have a good friend—a Realtor to whom I send absolutely every one of my first-time homebuyers. That's because he relates to them well, and he does a lot of business in the first-timer market. Other referrals may go to Realtors who specialize in luxury condos for older buyers.

Make sure you interview several candidates. They will also want to meet with you and find out what you're looking for regarding price range, amenities, and other features (such as being close to the baseball stadium or public transportation).

Realtors tend to specialize, and it's relatively easy to find one who specializes in condos. The best Realtors have the most listings and negotiate the most sales. So, unless you happen to know one, how do you find a top Realtor?

Visit a real estate office's website, where you can view their listings online. Look for the Realtors who have the most listings. Those are the top Realtors in that office.

Perform this exercise at a few Realtor websites. The names of the best Realtors will be prominent. Those are the ones you need to call.

Should you ignore someone who isn't the top-listed Realtor in the office? Of course not, but you don't want anyone who has been in the business for only a couple of years. Those agents haven't negotiated as many contracts as the more seasoned pros. The first few years of an agent's real estate career will determine whether he or she can make it in the industry or not. Agents get paid on straight commission; if they don't sell they don't eat. When you are talking with an agent who has 10 or more years' experience in real estate, you can trust that she is serious about the business and savvy enough to have weathered the various ups and downs of real estate cycles.

If real estate agents can survive a period when homes aren't selling, and make it to the next boom, they are not only good at real estate, but good at managing their business as well. If they weren't performing for their clients—again and again—they wouldn't have lasted this long.

A Realtor is also your personal adviser in a real estate transaction. He is there to help you negotiate your way through the offer stage, and more particularly to protect you when you navigate the sales contract.

Real estate contracts will vary by state. If you've never seen one, you can probably imagine that they're chock full of lawyer language, drawn up by attorneys whose job it is to protect the buyers and sellers as they come to an agreement.

If you were on your own—without a Realtor—and you made an offer, you'd make that offer to the listing agent (the seller's Realtor). The listing agent will fill out the contract for you, but he or she has absolutely no loyalty to you whatsoever. A listing agent's legal, binding obligation is to get the best deal for his or her client.

For instance, you make an offer, the seller accepts it, and in the sales contract there is a little box that says, "Buyer to Pay Title Insurance." The box is checked. You go along your merry way—only to find out that paying for *title insurance* isn't customary where you live, and the seller just hit you with an additional $2,000 in closing charges! Believe it or not, this happens every day.

On the other hand, if you had a Realtor working with you that wouldn't have happened. In all likelihood, the initial offer would have said something to the effect of, "Here's our offer at $300,000 and seller to pay all buyer's closing costs!"

BUYING FROM A DEVELOPER

The developer is the entity that started the entire condo project in the first place, from the ground up. The developer makes the plans, constructs the complex, hires a sales staff, handles the legal work around the CC&Rs, and takes on whatever else is necessary to facilitate the legal transfer of the properties to new owners.

Why do some developers build condos and townhouses while others build houses? Some of it has to do with individual areas of expertise. But it's also a matter of how and when developers get paid.

A builder of houses will get a contract on a home. After it's built, the buyer moves in and the builder moves on to the next home. But with condominiums and townhouses, the entire complex must be built before anyone can move in.

Buying from developers may also mean that you're required to use (or at least consult) some of their business affiliates such as lenders or *title* companies.

This is where you need to be on your toes. Developers can include language in the sales contract that says you must apply for a mortgage with a particular mortgage company. They can't force you to actually *use* their mortgage company, but they can insist that you at least apply.

There are business entities called *controlled business affiliations* (CBAs) and *affiliated business arrangements* (ABAs) that are created between various parties to work together and profit from a new development.

For example, the developer might have an ABA with a title company and a *mortgage broker*. This fact isn't hidden: When an ABA or a CBA exists, the salesperson you're buying the property from is required by federal statute to provide you with a disclosure that states, in essence, "Joe Developer and A Mortgage Company are partners and share the profits of this mortgage company."

There can be several reasons to form such alliances, but the bottom line is to have the ability to share in the profits of affiliated services. There's no harm in that. In fact, an ABA or a CBA has to be set up if the developer wants a piece of the mortgage and title insurance pie.

But why can't the mortgage company simply give the developers a referral fee each time a buyer closes a loan with them? Because referral fees between third parties are illegal. The Real Estate Settlement Procedures Act, or RESPA, requires that all monies changing hands from one party to another be disclosed to all parties, including the buyer and the seller. So, if someone sends a $1,000 referral fee that's not disclosed to all parties, he's in violation of federal law and can be fined, have his license taken away, or both.

One benefit of RESPA is that it prevents "steering" a buyer to a particular third party, say an *inspection* company, when the buyer thinks the agent is doing her a favor, but the agent is in fact receiving a silent referral fee (aka a kickback) for making the referral.

In such a case, is the referral tainted? Of course it is. You don't know whether the agent is referring an inspector who will work in the best interests of the buyer or is simply making some extra money on the side.

There is nothing inherently wrong with a CBA or an ABA.

But you do need to be on your guard in a big way. When buying directly from a developer, be sure your agent carefully reviews the contract so you'll be aware of these relationships.

A developer can sweeten the deal by providing certain incentives for you to use his or her mortgage operation to finance your condo. How sweet? Here's a common incentive from a developer.

"Get a mortgage loan from our company, and we'll pay for your title insurance policy!"

Depending on where you live and how large your loan, that title insurance policy could run you $3,000. We'll discuss title insurance costs in chapter 6. Still, $3,000 is hardly something to sneeze at. Why not use the builder's mortgage company if you can save $3,000?

Who do you think will ultimately pay that $3,000? Did the developer factor it into the sale price of the unit? Or do you think he's just a nice guy with a penchant for making less money on every transaction?

When you go to the closing you may notice the mortgage company's rates and fees are higher than everyone else's— about $3,000 higher. Do you think the mortgage company is going to work for free? *Loan officers* have to get paid. And of course there's plenty of overhead, as there is for every business.

I don't think the developer wants to give you $3,000. And I doubt the mortgage company wants to, either. These are businesses. And like all businesses, they're around to make money, not to give it away. That $3,000 can be accounted for either in the price of your property (which certainly could have been factored in from the very beginning) or in the price of your mortgage. That means it's you who pay the $3,000.

Are all such arrangements set up this way, where the incentive is built into the price of the property or you get charged more by the lender? No, they're not. In fact, many such ABAs offer discounted products and services as a part of the ABA—and that discount can be passed on to the buyers.

So how do you protect yourself from being taken advantage of? You need to make certain that the developer's mortgage company is offering competitive mortgage rates compared to other mortgage companies in the area. We'll discuss this tactic in more detail in chapter 3.

When buying from an individual and not a developer, there'll be no incentives to use other third-party services such as inspectors, appraisers, or mortgage companies. The seller might say something like, "If you need a good inspector call this guy," but really that's about it. It won't be something like, "If you use my mortgage company I'll pay you $3,000."

Another thing to watch out for when buying from a developer involves how the contract is worded when it comes to getting the loan approved. At some point in the negotiation process, sellers will want to see an approval letter from a lender to let them know you're serious about buying.

Sometimes, however, the language in the contract can put you between a rock and a hard place when it comes to your mortgage. For instance, say a new condo is being built. The sales office will write up sales contracts and the buyers will wait to move in until the condos are finished. The mortgage loan doesn't close until after all the units are completed, sometimes months after you've signed the sales contract. In this instance, you sign the contract, put down some earnest money as a deposit, apply for your mortgage, and wait.

Recall the incentive to apply for a mortgage at the developer's mortgage company. Sometimes the contract can read, "You agree that if you cannot obtain financing from other sources and our mortgage company issues an approval, you will accept financing from our mortgage company. If not, you will lose your earnest money deposit."

At first glance, that sounds fair enough. You can go anywhere you want to get financing. Why wouldn't you get an approval? And even if you didn't, why would one mortgage company approve when no one else approves your application?

I once received an e-mail from a buyer who was sorry that he had signed such a contract. He agreed to the wording that said if the developer's mortgage company got him an approval he would take the approval or forfeit his deposit money.

In this case, he did lose his deposit money, some $25,000 worth.

The buyer applied for the mortgage from the developer and at the same time got approved at his own bank. Now that he had his approval, he wouldn't need to worry about losing his deposit. Or would he?

As the condos were being built, he was also selling his own home. In fact, some of the funds to close would be coming from the sale of his property. In addition, his income was such that he could not afford both mortgages, so he had to sell his current home regardless of any down payment issues.

But his house didn't sell. He had it listed, but there were either no offers or the offers were too low. His bank's approval was contingent on his selling his current home.

The condos were days away from being finished. There was no way he could sell his house in time. So he asked for a letter from his bank saying he was no longer approved due to carrying two mortgages. He took the letter to the developer's mortgage company in the hope it would cancel his contract and return his deposit. The mortgage company said he couldn't have his money back because it had gotten his loan approved. He could either accept the approval or lose his money.

The buyer wanted to know how he got approved with such high debt-to-income numbers. The loan officer at the mortgage company said the approval was based on a *no documentation* loan. A no documentation loan means a loan where no income, no employment, and no debts are entered on the application. Debt figures aren't calculated whatsoever. Voila! Loan approval.

There was a catch: Mortgage rates on such loans are stratospheric, sometimes 2 or 3 percent higher than current mortgage rates. The higher rates help offset the risk of no documentation.

"But I can't afford two mortgages, much less another one with a higher rate!" claimed the buyer. And he was right. He couldn't afford the payments.

"Sorry," said the loan officer. "The contract doesn't say whether or not you can afford the mortgage. It says you must take our approved loan or lose your $25,000."

This actually happened. I don't recall exactly how he ended up, but I believe he sold his home for much less than the original asking price and took the original mortgage from his bank. It should be noted that not all contracts are written in such fashion. In fact, I hadn't seen one like that before. But the bottom line is that you (and your agent) must read the contract very carefully.

If you were still waffling on whether to use an agent to help you find a property and negotiate your contract, this should settle the matter.

| CHAPTER 3 |

Financing Your Condo, Co-op, or Townhouse the Right Way

Now to the good part: That's why you bought the book, right? This chapter identifies the various loan programs available for condos, co-ops, and townhouses, and it discusses how to evaluate them and pick the right loan for you.

If you pay any attention to all the mortgage commercials on television, the Web, and the radio, you'd think there are thousands of loan programs. But the fact is, mortgage loans are exactly the same from one lender to the next. That was done on purpose when the *Federal National Mortgage Association (Fannie Mae)* and the *Federal Home Loan Corporation (Freddie Mac)* were formed. The only real difference is how the various mortgage companies market them.

Fannie and Freddie are governmental agencies. They were formed by the U.S. government for the sole purpose of fostering homeownership. The way they foster homeownership is to buy mortgages from lenders so lenders can issue more mortgages. If you stop and think about it, it all makes sense.

If a lender has a million dollars in the bank and wants to lend money for homes, then after it lends that million, how will it continue to lend money on new homes? Easy: by selling the loans it already made.

But we're not talking about just any type of loan. It must conform to lending guidelines prescribed by Fannie and Freddie. If the loan meets the lending standards, then it can be bought and sold—sometimes over and over again, and sometimes to other lenders. This buying and selling activity is known as the "secondary" mortgage market.

The Federal Housing Administration, or FHA, also has lending guidelines, as does the Department of Veterans Affairs for *VA loans.* These loans, too, can be bought and sold.

So what does that mean when it comes to choosing among various loan packages? It means that behind all the marketing, behind the different names for loans, they're really all the same, just dressed up in different clothes.

Basically, there are two types of mortgages: fixed and adjustable.

FIXED-RATE MORTGAGES

Fixed-rate mortgages are loans with set monthly payments that never change: they're fixed. Buying and selling these loans won't change their nature. Once fixed, always fixed.

Fixed-rate terms can vary in length as determined by the

lender and selected by the borrower. Typically, the loans are issued in 5-year increments, beginning with a 10-year term. This 10-year period, during which the loan must be paid in full, is called the *amortization* period. Amortization periods are usually 30 years. That's what is meant by a "30-year fixed-rate mortgage." The interest rate never changes and the amortization period lasts for 30 years.

Perhaps the next most popular period is the 15-year loan. Other amortization periods are 10, 20, 25, and 40 years—and sometimes you'll find a lender issuing a 50-year loan.

Why the different periods? To some extent, to make it appear as though the consumer has a choice. It's the same fixed-rate loan; just the payback period is altered. The question is, which amortization period is right for you?

I don't believe there is a "best" payback period. In general, go with whatever feels comfortable to you, doesn't crimp your budget, and offers the lowest possible interest rate. The shorter the term, the less interest you will pay. At the same time, a short term means bigger monthly payments. When you begin to review loan offerings, you'll see 30-year and 15-year rates advertised. Be sure to take a close look at what those payments will be.

Let's look at the payments for 30-year and 15-year loans on the same $250,000.

Term	Rate	Payment
30 year	6.50%	$1,580
15 year	6.25%	$2,143

The 30-year payment is $563 lower than the 15-year rate. So

why doesn't everyone take the 30-year loan? After all, the payment is lower. Because when a loan is paid back over a shorter period of time, the interest rate is slightly lower (a 15-year fixed rate is normally about $1/4$ percent lower than its 30-year cousin). Let's look at the amount of mortgage interest paid over the life of the loan.

Term	Rate	Payment	Lifetime Interest
30 year	6.50%	$1,580	$318,000
15 year	6.25%	$2,143	$135,740

That's $182,260 out of your pocket. Okay, not exactly, because mortgage interest may be tax deductible. But it's an expense and an extended cost to borrowing money.

Another reason to compare amortization periods is to see if you'll qualify for the loan. Lenders rely on something called *debt ratio* (discussed later in this chapter) to determine whether you're eligible for a mortgage. Your debt ratio is simply the amount of your loan payment—including taxes and HOA fees—divided by your gross income. Let's take that same $250,000 loan and add some additional items to calculate debt ratio.

30 year	
Payment	$1,580
Taxes	$ 200
HOA	$ 200
Total	$1,980

A common debt ratio for housing expenses is around 30 percent. So, in this instance a lender would say that your monthly income would need to be around $6,600 to qualify for the loan.

Now examine the 15-year loan.

15 year	
Payment	$2,143
Taxes	$ 200
HOA	$ 200
Total	$2,543

The qualifying income for the 15-year loan would be $8,476, or $1,876 more than the 30-year loan. That's a lot of money! And that's why people tend to choose the 30-year over the 15-year loan. The payment is not only lower, but it helps them qualify for the loan, too.

Paying less interest over the life of the loan is a good idea, but some buyers fear the 15-year payment schedule is out of reach. There are two alternatives: different amortization periods and prepayments.

Different Amortization Periods

Just because the lender doesn't advertise a 20-year loan doesn't mean it doesn't offer one. The same goes for 25-year and 40-year loans. But you have to ask your loan officer. Why ask? Because you can in fact get closer to your goal of paying as little interest as possible while making sure the monthly payment feels comfortable to you and you can qualify. Let's examine the interest paid over the life of the loan with a few different amortization periods.

Term	Rate	Payment	Lifetime Interest
40 year	6.75%	$1,508	$473,840
30 year	6.50%	$1,580	$318,000
25 year	6.50%	$1,688	$256,400
20 year	6.25%	$1,827	$188,480
15 year	6.25%	$2,143	$135,740
10 year	6.25%	$2,807	$ 86,840

Changing amortization periods will have a dramatic effect on your payments and your interest paid. Clients who select a 15-year loan are often shocked at how high the payment would be. I always suggest looking at 20-year and 25-year loans along with a 30-year fixed loan. There are just a handful of lenders that offer even longer periods, but I would not recommend a 50-year loan. It's simply too much in interest. But even with a longer amortization period, you can also save on interest by prepaying the *note*. Prepaying the note means paying down the *principal* balance ahead of time.

Prepayments

You can prepay a loan down any time you wish. Some loans carry a *prepayment penalty* should you pay down the mortgage ahead of time. But typically those penalties are charged on loans for people with damaged credit.

One of the loan documents you will sign when applying for a mortgage is the Truth in Lending Form, or TIL. This form has lots of numbers and boxes on it, but one of the boxes toward the end of the form states: *This loan does/does not have a prepayment penalty.*

If there is a prepayment penalty it can be assessed in two ways: hard or soft. A hard penalty means you can't, under any circumstances, pay any part of the note ahead of time without paying the penalty. A typical penalty is six months worth of interest. Hard penalties used to be more common than they are today. In fact, they're becoming extremely rare. A soft penalty is a loan that doesn't charge you a prepayment penalty if you:

> ➤ Sell the home
> ➤ Pay no more than 20 percent of the balance during any 12-month period
> ➤ Keep the loan more than three years

This means that although there are a few prepayment penalty–type loans out there, they are not nearly as common as they were just a few years ago. In most cases, you can pay ahead any time.

This is a good option for those who really want to reduce the interest paid over the life of the loan but can't afford the 15-year payment. For those, a good strategy is to take the pay down of a 30-year amortization period as though it were a 15-year loan.

In this example, you'd pay the $563 difference each month on top of your regular 30-year fixed-rate payment. Most lenders have a line or a box on the mortgage statement where you enter in the amount extra you're paying.

Some months when unexpected expenses arise and you don't want to make the extra payment, you have the luxury of making the standard payment.

When you pay down a fixed-rate mortgage, your monthly

payment amount won't ever go down. Remember, it's fixed for the life of the loan. You're reducing the loan term. If you make the extra $563 payment each month, you'll find that your loan is paid off in 15 years, not 30.

There is another method of prepayment to reduce the term of the loan: biweekly. A biweekly program is a method where monthly payments toward the principal balance are paid every other week instead of once per month.

If you desire to reduce your mortgage with this method, I suggest taking one payment amount, dividing it by 12 and then making that payment each month. At the end of the year, you'll have made one extra mortgage payment. This can shorten the term by five or six years.

Biweekly programs are often marketed to homeowners by firms that charge a set-up fee. But it's actually something you can do yourself without paying the fee.

ADJUSTABLE-RATE MORTGAGE

In an *adjustable-rate mortgage*, or ARM, the interest rate can change (or adjust) periodically throughout the life of the loan.

Fortunately, the adjustment procedures are built into the note itself; your mortgage rate won't change at the whim of your lender. What are the adjustment procedures? Adjustments are based on the index, margin, adjustment cap, and lifetime cap.

The *index* is the starting point for how your monthly payments will adjust due to the change in the ARM. The index, or the base point, is tied to a specific number associated with a commonly tracked financial number.

Common indexes are the one-year Treasury note and the *London Interbank Offered Rate,* or *LIBOR.* There have been other indexes in the past, but these two are by far the most common.

A *margin* is the amount, expressed as a percent, that is added to the initial index. Common margins range from 2.00 percent to 2.75 percent.

The *adjustment cap* is a consumer piece that protects the mortgage rate from wild swings, hampering the borrower's ability to pay the note. After adding the index to the margin, this cap allows for only incremental increases when the rate adjusts. Caps are based on the previous mortgage rate. If the rate for the past year was 5 percent, then that rate can go no higher than the annual cap will allow, regardless of the index.

Caps can also apply when mortgage rates go down. Indexes can go up or down; they don't always have to go up.

The *lifetime cap* is the mortgage rate's limit over the course of the loan. It is based on the initial starting rate of the adjustable-rate mortgage.

Typically, about 60 days before an adjustable-rate mortgage makes an adjustment—sometimes called a "reset"—the lender will notify the borrower. Adjustment dates can be annual, twice per year, or even monthly. But most ARMs adjust either once or twice per year.

The lender letter will advise you of the index to be used and will add the margin to establish your new rate for the following year, in the case of a one-year ARM, for instance.

If the ARM is based on the one-year Treasury bill, the lender will use the then-current yield for the one-year Treasury. If the index on that day is 3.00 percent, the lender will add the margin of, say, 2.50 percent. By adding the margin and the index together, your rate for the following year will be 3.00 + 2.50 = 5.50 percent. Moving forward, the cap will protect you from wild swings if the index experiences a large increase (or decrease).

For example, say the one-year Treasury bill was indexed at 2 percent, but due to inflationary concerns over the life of the loan (we'll examine in detail how mortgage rates move in the next section), the one-year Treasury has hit 5 percent.

Now, at the time of adjustment, the lender would take the then-current 5.00 percent rate and add the 2.50 percent margin. The new rate would be 7.50 percent.

However, because the previous year's rate was 4.50 percent, the adjustment cap keeps it from going up no more than 2.00 percent from the previous year's rate. The lender would love the rate to go to 7.50 percent, but due to the cap it can go only to 6.50 percent.

Common lifetime caps are 5 percent or 6 percent. At 5 percent, the highest your rate could ever go would be 10 percent. Even if the one-year Treasury hit 12 percent, your mortgage rate would never go higher than 10 percent, your lifetime cap.

THE HYBRID

One variation of an ARM—known as a "hybrid"—is a cross between a fixed rate and an adjustable rate. The loan is fixed for the first few years at a predetermined rate and term; and then it turns into an annual or six-month ARM.

Hybrids start out slightly higher than an ARM but lower than a fixed rate. It's a "tweener."

Because it is an ARM, the hybrid has an index, a margin, and caps, but it doesn't adjust until after the initial fixed period.

Hybrids have different names based on the length of the fixed period and what the rate will adjust to. For example, a $3/1$ ARM means the ARM is fixed for three years, then turns into a one-year ARM. A $5/1$ ARM means the ARM is fixed for five years, then turns into a one-year ARM.

A twist is the $5/6$ ARM. At first glance one would think that this hybrid is fixed for five years, then adjusts every six years. But in reality it's fixed for five years, then adjusts every six months.

There are $3/1$, $5/1$, $7/1$, and even $10/1$ hybrids. And there can be $3/6$, $5/6$, $7/6$, and $10/6$ hybrids, although the most common are the $3/1$ and $5/1$ and the $3/6$ and $5/6$.

Hybrids, like their ARM cousins, have both adjustment and lifetime caps. Caps on both hybrids and ARMs are expressed as a series of numbers such as $2/1/6$ or $2/2/6$.

The first number is the percentage cap for the first adjustment; the second number is the annual or semiannual cap; and the last number is the lifetime cap. For a $2/1/6$, the initial cap of

2 percent above the original start rate adjusts annually (one year) and has a 6 percent lifetime cap.

Adjustments occur when the fixed-rate period expires and the hybrid performs like an ordinary ARM. For instance, on a 3/6 hybrid, at the end of three years the loan would take the index, add the margin to it, and then reset for the following six months, with the caps limiting the adjustment up or down.

Why would anyone choose an ARM? ARMs typically come with an initial start rate, or a "teaser" rate that can be 1 to 2 percent lower than the *fully indexed rate* (the rate arrived at by adding the index and the margin).

This is to entice the consumer to select an ARM over a fixed rate because of the ARM's lower starting rate. Lenders like ARMs. And why wouldn't they? As interest rates change over the course of the years, the ARM is tied to the current costs of money, plus a margin over that. As rates fluctuate, ARMs fluctuate with them, with the lender less likely to lose money over the term of the loan.

With a fixed rate, the rate is locked in until the note is retired.

So which is best for you—a fixed-rate mortgage, an ARM, or a hybrid? There are two things to consider: current market rates and how long you intend to keep the property.

Interest rates change over the course of months and years. Sometimes they'll be relatively high and sometimes they'll be historically low. In the early 1980s, for instance, mortgage rates were around 20 percent! Twenty years later, they hit historical lows in the 5 percent range.

By comparing current market rates with historical rates,

you can determine if the market is at a relative high, a relative low, or somewhere in the middle. You can find historical rate charts on the Internet. Personally, I visit www.hsh.com when I want to look at various indexes and rate trends.

Simply, if rates are relatively high, you may want to take an ARM. And if rates are relatively low, you'd want to *lock* in those low rates for the long term, so you'd select a fixed rate.

You would select an ARM because its initial teaser rate is lower than the current fixed rate offerings—and because the ARM's rate will adjust downward as interest rates move lower. Then—if you plan on owning the property and keeping the mortgage long term—when rates hit rock bottom you would *refinance* that note into a fixed-rate mortgage.

If you don't plan to keep the property for more than a few years, you should consider either an ARM or a hybrid. People take these loans when they're fairly certain they'll be transferred and will have to sell the property in the short term.

For instance, say you know you're going to be transferred in four years and you want to own, not rent. You may want to consider a 5/1 ARM with a lower start rate than a fixed one. Your payments would be lower and you wouldn't have to worry about a reset because, according to your plans, you would have sold the condo before the initial fixed-rate period expires.

When you're deciding between an ARM and a hybrid, you need to compare both programs over the projected time frame during which you would own the home. Let's look at an example—a $250,000 loan with a 5/1 hybrid at 5.75 percent and a one-year ARM based on the one-year Treasury bill with a teaser rate of 4.75 percent, 2 percent annual caps, and a 2.75 margin. And let's assume a worst-case scenario: that you will hit the 2 percent annual cap at each reset.

Year	ARM	Hybrid ARM	Savings (annual)
1	$1,304	$1,458	$1,848
2	$1,621	$1,458	($2,724)

Did you see what happened? All gains won by the ARM during the first year were wiped out by losses in the second year. Granted, we did play the worst-case scenario, where the fully indexed rate would "cap out" and go from 4.75 percent to 6.75 percent. But the risk is still there.

ARMs give you a teaser rate. You need to do some serious homework and consult your loan officer as to the proper mortgage program for you. But if you're short term, a hybrid with a low teaser rate is the better choice.

One last note on ARMs and hybrids: When lenders evaluate your ability to pay the mortgage, they will look at your gross monthly income and the fully indexed rate with an ARM or 2 percent above the start rate for a hybrid.

For example, a lender will not use a 4.75 percent teaser rate to qualify you. Instead it uses the then-current index plus the margin. If the index is 5.00 percent and the margin is 2.75 percent, then the lender will use 7.75 percent as your qualifying rate.

OPTION ARMs AND NEGATIVE AMORTIZATION

Before we end our discussion on adjustable-rate mortgages, I want to mention two characteristics of some potentially

bad loan features—*payment-option ARMs* and *negative amortization.*

Payment-option ARMs—sometimes called "option ARMs"
or "pay-option ARMs"—have a series of payment choices built
right into the loan program itself. Those options include the
contract or initial pay rate, an interest-only plan, a fully indexed
plan, and a fixed-rate plan all rolled into one loan.

It sounds confusing. And for the average buyer it is.

The contract or initial pay rate can be super low: 3 percent,
2 percent, or even 1 percent. It has an index and a margin just
like any other ARM; and each month you actually have a choice
of which to pay. You have a pay option. Let's look at a typical
scenario where you could pay a $250,000 loan amount.

Rate/type	Payment
1%	$ 804
5.75% interest only	$ 1,197
5.75% fully amortized	$ 1,458
6.25% 30-year fixed	$ 1,539

So who would pay the 30-year fixed rate or the 5.75 percent
fully amortized rate? Why wouldn't everyone just pay the initial
pay rate or the interest-only rate? Because of negative amortization.

These loans have potential for the loan to negatively amor-
tize, or actually grow rather than get smaller. The trick on these
loans is that when you pay the 1 percent rate, the lender compares that to a fully amortized rate payment. If you don't pay at
least the fully amortized payment, then the difference between

the initial rate and the fully amortized rate gets added back to your original loan amount. That's not good.

Such loans have been around for decades, but until recently were they weren't promoted much to the general public. They're not inherently evil. They weren't designed to take away homeowners' *equity*. Rather, they can be viewed more as a financial management tool.

For instance, these loans could make sense when the borrower gets paid irregularly or receives a large annual bonus. The buyer could pay the minimum payment and make up for it when he gets his bonus or hits a big payday, erasing any potential for long-term loan growth.

Nonetheless, with all the loan choices out there, this is one simply to stay away from. Period.

HOW MORTGAGE RATES ARE SET

The Federal Reserve Board (Fed) sets rates, right? You just follow the Fed's moves, wait for the rates to drop, and then you buy, right? Wrong. Dead wrong. In fact, you might find that rates are higher *after* the Fed cut. I know it's a bit counterintuitive but let's discover how mortgage rates are really set and how to take advantage of lower rates in the future.

More important, knowing how mortgage rates are set will help you when negotiating interest rates with your loan officer.

Fixed mortgage rates are tied to what's called a *mortgage bond*, or *mortgage-backed security*. They're like any other bond, such as a 30-year Treasury bond or a corporate bond; and traders buy and sell them all day long. It's this index to which fixed rates are set, not by what the Fed does or does not do.

Fixed rates will anticipate the Fed's actions but not react to them.

So first, exactly what is a bond?

It's a piece of paper you buy that has a fixed return at the end of a certain period of time. Think of a U.S. government savings bonds. When you buy a $100 savings bond, it doesn't cost $100, it costs $50. At the end of the savings bond's term, typically 17 years, you may cash it in for $100, even though you only paid $50 for it.

Your $50 investment will result in a $100 return. Eventually. But while you're waiting for the bond to mature, lots can happen, economically speaking. Inflation is particularly important during that waiting period.

If after 17 years, things simply cost more due to inflation, that $100 won't be worth as much as it was originally. Bonds aren't a very sexy investment. They pay less, but they're relatively safe.

Each morning, the trading boards open up for the day's mortgage bond activity. There is a Fannie Mae bond, a bond for government-backed loans such as FHA and VA mortgages, and other similar mortgage bonds.

As mortgage bonds trade throughout the day, investors make long-term and short-term bets on the economy. When the economy is slow, investors pull their money out of riskier investments such as stocks and put it into bonds and other safer investments. The increased demand pushes up the price for such investments. In the simple example of the $100 savings bond, instead of costing $50, the bond might cost $51. When the price of a mortgage bond goes up, the yield is decreased. That yield is the rate of return on that bond. In everyday language, that means mortgage rates will fall during slower economic times.

When the economy is back on track and humming right along, investors pull money out of lower-yielding bonds and put it into the stock market. When the price of the mortgage bond falls, the yield has to increase. That means mortgage rates rise.

The Fed does control certain interest rates including the Federal Funds rate, which is the rate at which banks can borrow from one another on an overnight basis. Why do banks borrow from one another on such short notice? *Reserves.*

At the end of every business day, a bank is required to have a minimum amount of cash in its vaults to cover its accounts. If a bank lends money, it needs to make sure it has enough to cover consumer-demand accounts such as checking and savings. If the bank doesn't have enough cash on hand, it will make arrangements to borrow from other banks. This is the rate the Fed moves up, down, or leaves the same when it meets every six weeks.

So when you hear that the Fed cut interest rates, don't think that your mortgage rate is also being reduced.

The Fed manipulates the federal funds rate to control an overheated economy or stimulate a sluggish one. When an economy is slowing, the Fed may reduce the federal funds rate. This enables banks to lend money to businesses that may want to expand their operations or produce more goods.

If the economy is overheated and inflation is starting to creep in due to consumer demand, the Fed tries to keep a lid on inflation by raising rates to slow growth. Monitoring the economy is a never-ending job.

HOW LENDERS SET THEIR RATES

Each business day, mortgage companies set rates for their customers. Lenders have what is called a "secondary department" whose job is to set rates according to market conditions while keeping competitive with other mortgage companies.

Mortgage rates are typically released around 11:00 A.M. EST each day, after the major economic reports are released. These economic reports can indicate whether an economy is slowing, growing, or remaining stable.

If a report is released showing that more people are unemployed than anticipated, then it's likely that mortgage rates will fall a bit for that day. When more people are out of work, it suggests that the economy isn't doing very well.

If economic reports are released indicating that the economy is indeed slowing or even heading into a recession, then rates will continue to fall. If the slowing trend continues over the course of a few months, then mortgage rates will see an extended decline.

If, on the contrary, reports show more people at work or more housing starts and retail sales are up, then mortgage rates will rise.

Secondary departments have to make prudent, educated

decisions every day on how to price their mortgage rates. Sometimes they'll even make a rate change during the course of a business day.

There are bonds for 30-year fixed rates, for 15-year fixed rates, and so on. Though there are literally thousands of places to get a mortgage, they all index their mortgages from the very same mortgage bond.

Adjustable-rate mortgages are not tied to mortgage bonds, but to the index the adjustable rate is tied to (as mentioned in the previous section). There is one exception: loans tied to the *Wall Street Journal* prime rate.

The *prime rate* is determined by a *survey* of the 30 largest banks in the United States. It is the rate banks typically charge their very best customers to borrow money. The prime rate will be set at 3 percentage points above the *Fed funds rate*. If the Fed funds rate were at 5 percent, the prime rate would be 8 percent. This is the only condo loan type that is tied directly to the Fed. Prime rates are typically found on equity loans, not on mortgages used to buy property. We'll discuss equity loans for condos a little later in this chapter.

TYPES OF MORTGAGE LENDERS

It used to be that mortgages came from a Savings and Loan, but that changed in the late 1980s when the Savings and Loan crisis hit and the federal government was charged with buying out failed Savings and Loans. Later, mortgage banks began issuing mortgages, filling the void left by the defunct Savings and Loan companies. Soon thereafter, mortgage brokers became more prevalent. Nowadays, you can get a mortgage from your bank down the street, your credit union, a mortgage banker, a mortgage broker, a correspondent lender, or an online lender. How do you decide which is best for you?

Retail Bank

A retail bank is where you keep your checking or savings account. It's right down the street and offers everything from credit cards to student loans to, that's right, your mortgage.

Your retail bank may not have the absolute lowest interest rate, but it may offer incentives such as waiving various bank fees or giving you a free safety deposit box.

Credit Union

A credit union is similar to a bank: It offers mostly the same products and services as a retail bank, but it's open only to members. A university may have its own credit union, for example. Or one may be open to those who live in a certain area or who are employed at the same company.

Credit unions will rarely make a mortgage loan directly. Instead, they will act as mortgage brokers or they will contract with a third-party lender to place mortgage loans for them. Credit union mortgage rates are typically very competitive, just as they are with other types of consumer loans.

Mortgage Banker

Mortgage bankers do one thing and one thing only: they issue mortgage loans. A mortgage banker does not issue credit cards or other consumer credit services.

Theoretically, with this singular focus, the mortgage banker can be more competitive and more efficient than a retail bank with its multiple profit centers, products, and services.

When a mortgage banker places a mortgage loan, it typically has a credit line established somewhere to fund the mortgage being placed. If you have a $250,000 mortgage, the mortgage banker will either open up its cash vault or transfer $250,000 from its credit line to the seller of the property.

Mortgage bankers can keep your loan or sell it. When they keep your loan, you will send them your monthly mortgage payments. Collecting monthly mortgage payments is called "servicing."

When a mortgage banker sells your mortgage, nothing changes with the mortgage itself. You'll be sending your monthly payment to a new mortgage company that will service your loan.

Most lenders buy and sell mortgages all the time. It is rare for a mortgage lender never to sell a mortgage. But there is a federal law that requires lenders to tell you what percent of loans they have sold in the past. You'll find that information on the Servicing Disclosure form. There will be different boxes that say:

"Last year we sold ❑ 0–25%, ❑ 26–50%, ❑ 51–75%, ❑ 76–100% of our loans."

And one of those boxes should be checked.

Before buying and selling loans in the *secondary market* became more common in the 1990s, borrowers were not used to their loan being sold—and some took it personally. I recall a mortgage that I got from a mortgage bank that later sold it to my very own bank. I suddenly received a lot of freebies because I had a credit card, checking and savings accounts, and now a mortgage at the same bank.

My bank kept my mortgage for about a year, then sold it to someone else.

Mortgage bankers take the mortgage from cradle to grave. In other words, you will apply directly with them, and your loan will be processed and approved by the lender, who will supply the funds at the closing table.

Mortgage Broker

Mortgage brokers are by far the single largest source for mortgages and, depending on which data you read, account for about half of all the mortgages generated in the United States.

Mortgage brokers don't have any mortgage money, but they find other lenders who do. A mortgage broker works with different banks to place loans, much like an independent insurance agent works with different insurance companies to get policies for his clients.

Brokers compare different mortgage rates from different mortgage companies and match up the buyers with the rates. Sometimes they will find a mortgage company that offers a particular product not found at most other mortgage companies.

Brokers take mortgage applications from buyers, but they do not approve loans. Instead, a broker will document the loan application with everything the lender needs to approve the loan, including things such as the borrower's pay stubs, bank statements, and W2 forms.

When the file is documented, the broker sends the loan over to the mortgage bank, which will approve the loan, order the closing papers, and provide the funds at closing.

Does that make mortgage brokers more expensive because they add another layer to the costs? No, because mortgage brokers represent the wholesale division of a mortgage bank.

Most major banks have separate divisions—known as "wholesale divisions"—that cater to mortgage brokers. These wholesale operations approve mortgage loans sent to them by mortgage brokers. Wholesale lenders also hire sales staff and customer service people that make sales calls on mortgage brokers, take them to lunch, and help them when there are problems with loans that are in process. And lenders offer mortgage loans at a discount to the broker who in turn "marks up" the interest rate to compete with retail banks, credit unions, and mortgage bankers.

Lenders can offer loans on a wholesale basis because mortgage brokers do most of the "heavy lifting" and absorb a good portion of the overhead.

By eliminating a significant portion of a mortgage operation's expenses (staff, office space, utilities, etc.) and placing it on the shoulders of a mortgage broker, a bank can save enough money to offer these discounts to brokers.

Wholesale lenders price their loans the same way as any other mortgage company: by issuing new rates every day based on current market conditions and the price of mortgage bonds that day.

So which is better, a banker or a broker?

I began my career in real estate finance as a broker in California. Then I worked for a mortgage bank in Texas before starting my own business. So I know how each works from the inside.

By its nature, a broker does indeed have the ability to shop around for the absolute best interest rate, but there are a couple of caveats. The first is that because lenders price their mortgages on the same index, one lender's rate can't be wildly different from another's. When I would scour the various wholesale lenders' rate sheets, I never saw one lender at 6 percent while others were at 7 percent. It can't happen that way. If you see rates vary by that much, then something's wrong. Either someone made a mistake or you're being misled.

I did see variances, but they were marginal. Sometimes one lender would come in $1/8$ percent lower than other lenders, but no lender was consistently $1/4$ percent lower than anyone else.

Occasionally, in an attempt to gain market share a lender will essentially "give away" mortgages to increase volume. But that never lasts for very long. Lenders take it on the chin to boost volume and then ratchet the rates back up to meet their competitors. Wholesale mortgage companies subscribe to various rate-reporting services that tell them what their competitors are charging.

Most likely a mortgage broker will see a short list of lenders who offer the very same rate, but with minor differences in points. (We'll discuss points in detail in chapter 6.) Lender A may offer 6 percent at $1/2$ point while Lender B would offer 6 percent at $5/8$ of a point, for instance. Even when these rates are attractive, a broker will shop around for a better deal—for him, not for you.

A mortgage broker can also search for different loan types that appeal to a certain segment of borrowers—or loans made available by certain banks but not others. This typically isn't the case with mortgage loans because the bulk of mortgages fall into *conventional loan* categories, such as Fannie Mae and Freddie Mac insured loans or government loans under FHA or VA programs.

Sometimes when a mortgage bank doesn't offer a certain product, a mortgage broker will find one that does. For example, a mortgage bank may not offer a loan for a condo in a high-rise complex of more than 25 stories. Or a bank doesn't want to finance properties for investors who will rent them out instead of living in them. A broker can have a list of "niche" loan programs and know exactly where a specialty loan needs to be placed. A loan officer for a mortgage bank doesn't have the luxury of going to a list of wholesale lenders and calling them for a special loan program.

Bankers do, however, have a key ingredient that brokers simply do not: control over the loan file. Loan approval times are shorter with a banker than with a broker simply because there are fewer steps the loan needs to go through to get to the closing table.

When a broker delivers a loan file to a wholesale lender, the loan is literally handed off and the broker sits back and waits. When there is a question or a problem with a loan submitted by the broker, the lender's underwriter doesn't call the mortgage broker with the problem. Instead, she'll note what the problem is in the file and then send the file back to the account executive or customer service representative at the mortgage company, who then contacts the loan officer. When the problem is resolved, the process begins all over again with the application going back up the ladder for the underwriter to review. This process may take several days. On the other hand, a mortgage banker would have the underwriter talk to the loan officer or processor and get the issue resolved directly.

Correspondent Lender

There is a special class of mortgage banks that find, process, approve, and fund loans but can also act like a mortgage broker by shopping around for the best rate or a particular loan program. These operations are known as *correspondent lenders*.

A correspondent lender will make an agreement ahead of time to sell a loan at a particular rate and at a particular time. Meanwhile, the correspondent lender has agreements with other mortgage banks that offer rates and programs at wholesale prices. Just as a broker can have several wholesale lenders from which to select, a mortgage banker may have several correspondent channels that offer the very same loans that mortgage brokers can find.

I believe this is the best choice—a mortgage bank with multiple correspondent relationships. These mortgage companies combine the control inherent in a mortgage bank with multiple sources for rates and loan programs.

It's difficult to tell by the name of a company if it's a banker, a correspondent, or a broker. You can do some research on the company's website. The site will tell you whether the company is a broker or a direct lender. But *correspondent bankers* won't have such a description. You'll have to call them up and ask directly if they're mortgage bankers—and so, do they also have the ability to shop around for a better rate?

If you can find a correspondent banker, that would get my vote in the broker versus banker match up.

Online Lender

I didn't mention this at the outset, but I do want to address a couple of items concerning online lenders. First, an online lender is not simply a mortgage company with a website. Every mortgage company has a website.

An online lender is a business that has no building or physical presence in your area but does have a website dedicated to mortgage lending. You apply online and work with customer service people who are employed by the lender.

When you apply online, the lender begins to process your loan and you send the requested documents by fax, mail, or e-mail. When there are questions, you talk with the customer people directly, but you never meet them in person.

Many stock brokerages and investment advisers offer online mortgage operations as a service to their investor clients. If you feel comfortable working completely online with a customer service representative, it's ok, but I wouldn't recommend it to someone who could use a little handholding or doesn't understand the mortgage process.

If there's a problem with the loan application or there's a question that needs to be resolved, an online lender can at times hinder more than help. Sometimes the customer service representative does not fully understand the issue. Sometimes the rep doesn't know about local laws and statutes affecting the buyer.

And your customer service person or online loan officer probably isn't the most knowledgeable in the field. The best loan officers get paid a lot because they know the business inside and out and can guide someone effortlessly through the loan process.

HOW TO FIND THE BEST LOAN OFFICER

If you know the type of lender you want to work with, or if you've determined that either a banker or a broker is fine with you, then what you're looking for at this stage is the best loan officer you can find. And that can be a tall order, especially if you're new in town and don't know a lot of people.

Loan officers are the individuals who help guide you through the loan process, who quote you interest rates, and who are there when you have mortgage questions. Whether you're working with a banker or a lender, your loan officer is the most important person to you at the mortgage company.

Think about that for a moment. A mortgage company can spend millions on promotional material or marketing campaigns—and it takes just one lousy loan officer to mess it up for them. A mortgage company, just like any other company, can only be as good as the people it hires. But a good loan officer will be responsive, be experienced, and make good money.

Finding responsiveness in a loan officer is one of the easiest tests when you first start to look for a loan. Place a few calls or send out some e-mails, then wait and see who calls you back and when. I've heard customers tell me that some loan officers didn't even return a phone call after a week! Is that the kind of customer service you want?

If a loan officer doesn't call you back in a timely manner for something as important as getting new business (your loan), then how do you think he'll perform when the loan actually gets in the door?

Loan officers who use PDAs such as a BlackBerry or Treo do so because they want to give the best service they possibly can. They want their customers to know they can get hold of their loan officer any time they have a question—nights, weekends, whenever. Customers know that if they send an e-mail or leave a voice mail, the loan officer will receive it.

Experience is also important. The best loan officers have been around for 10 years or more. They know the lending business inside and out.

By early in the year 2000, technology had really taken hold of the industry. Automated underwriting is an electronic method of issuing a loan approval. Today, Fannie Mae and

Freddie Mac lenders use them on all their loans. Here's how it works: A client visits a loan office's website and completes a loan application; or a loan officer takes the loan application directly from the client. The loan officer reviews the application, then submits the loan for approval using automated underwriting. After a few seconds, the preapproval comes back, along with a laundry list of items the loan officer needs to collect from the buyer.

It's pretty easy, actually. Especially compared to manually processing and approving a mortgage loan. When processing a mortgage loan, the loan officer puts the file together knowing ahead of time that the loan is likely to be approved or not, based on income, credit, title review, and *appraisal* reports.

Before there was automated underwriting, the loan officer functioned almost like an underwriter. Before the loan was submitted for approval, she had to determine whether or not the loan was "approvable." That meant that the loan officer had to know her stuff (such as documentation guidelines, debt ratios guidelines, and credit—way before *credit scores* were used).

In other words, a loan officer who depends on an *automated underwriting* system may not fully understand why that loan did or did not get approved. The loan officer just inputs all the data and pushes a button. But if there is a problem or the loan isn't approved, bad things can happen.

Loan officers who rely on automated underwriting without understanding underwriting may be a hindrance. Generally, they are new to the business and don't know how loans are approved. They function more like salespeople than counselors who can give thorough advice.

Generally speaking, someone who has been in the business for 10 or more years has the experience, the tenacity, and the ability to manage his or her business properly and weather the ups and downs in the mortgage business. But at the very least, look for a loan officer with a minimum of five years' experience.

Every state in the union has some sort of mortgage licensing requirement, but the bar is set pretty low. Nearly anyone can meet the requirements. It's the experience that counts.

If a loan officer makes good money, this means she's doing something right. She's successful and manages a good business. Most loan officers are on straight commission. That of course means "no loans, no paycheck."

Loan officers who work in their bank lobby or customer service people at a 1-800 number receive a salary and a small commission. The small commission is because it's the bank, not the loan officer, that brings in business. The loan officer isn't out there building her own business by establishing relationships with real estate agents, builders, and previous clients.

You're certainly not going to ask, "By the way, how much money do you make?" Instead you'll have to make your best guess. As a rule of thumb, anyone who can stay in the mortgage business for at least a five-year stint has probably established a good base of business that keeps her from getting out of the industry.

Maybe there are plaques and awards on her office wall. Maybe her business card shows that she has achieved a certain level of production. I used to work with a bank-owned mortgage company where the top producers won the "Presidents

Club" award if they averaged a million dollars in production every month.

Okay, so if these are the qualities you want in a loan officer, well, where in the heck are the good ones? Doesn't it seem as though every loan officer advertises great rates and great service? Of course. Who would advertise terrible rates and terrible service?

If you're currently working with a Realtor, ask him for a list of loan officers he has worked with in the past and start your journey there. Top Realtors have reputations to maintain. They need support teams who can make their jobs easier while making the Realtors look good.

Top loan officers solicit the business of top Realtors. Loan officers who regularly close $20 to $30 million or more a year are typically on top Realtors' short lists. They get there by getting the job done, and by keeping the buyers happy all the way to the closing table.

Top loan officers know the business inside and out. They get referred because Realtors know buyers will be in good hands. Top loan officers provide excellent customer service, and they offer competitive mortgage programs. They know that if they screw up a deal or do something untoward, not only will they lose that business from the Realtor, but they'll earn bad reputations among other Realtors in that office as well.

If you don't know of a good Realtor, find one who has lots of listings. Visit his website, look for a section about mortgages, and see if there are loan officers listed there. You'll notice that Realtors don't list mortgage companies; they list loan officers who work at mortgage companies.

After you find one top Realtor, find another and perhaps another. If you notice a particular loan officer's name popping up with more regularity than some others, you'll know you have a winner.

It's also important to find out if you and a loan officer are "a good fit" for each other. Personality can come into play in any business relationship. Goodness knows there are different personality traits. Some people are aggressive, some are direct and to the point, and others are more passive and conversational. If your goal is to find the absolute best loan officer, then you must keep personality in the mix. You can do this by calling the loan officers on the phone, asking a few questions, and seeing how you feel afterward. What questions should you ask? Here are a few that should be included: How long have you been in the business? How long have you worked at your current company? and What Realtors do you work with?

Now, narrow your choices down to the two loan officers who impressed you the most.

HOW TO FIND THE BEST RATE

You know how mortgage rates are actually set. You know the different types of mortgage companies. And you've located some good loan officers. Now it's time to apply all that knowledge and find the best mortgage rate for your new condo, townhouse, or co-op. It's time to find your rate and select your loan officer.

Hold Your Ground

In your quest for the best rate, the first thing you need to do is hold your ground. Once you've decided on the loan program that is right for you—a 20-year fixed rate, for instance—don't be tempted to change programs during your rate search. If you do, you'll have to start the search process all over again. Why?

Let's say that a mortgage company likes to push its ARM programs. There are certain "scripts" that loan officers can follow to promote a particular loan program—and some can be pretty convincing. Other loan officers take seminars on how to "pitch" a mortgage program so that it looks different or acts differently from other loan programs.

When you make your phone calls, you're shopping for rates. Mortgage companies, however, aren't all that competitive for fixed-rate loans. But they are very competitive with adjustable-rate programs.

"Well, we do have a 20-year loan program, but have you looked at our 7/1 hybrid? How long do you think you'll own that unit? Did you know that people don't keep a mortgage for 20 years? They either refinance or sell long before then, so why pay more for a mortgage program that you won't need when our 7/1 ARM can save you? Blah, blah, blah."

Sometimes these scripts are dead-on; they make lots of sense. But remember that mortgage companies price their loans from the very same indexes. One mortgage company can't have something that another one doesn't have.

For instance, say that you've done your research and are going out to buy a particular mountain bike. You know the model and the make and all the accessories. You take your information with you to a bicycle shop and ask for their rock bottom price. The salesman tells you $579, delivered and assembled.

You then go to the next bicycle shop and find the exact same mountain bike and ask for their lowest price. The salesman, knowing their prices are a bit higher than their competitors, tells you the price is $619, but then starts asking a few questions:

"How often do you ride and on what type of trails? Will there be lots of rocky trails that might damage your tires? If not, why not look at another model with the same features, but built for the casual mountain biker? It's only $519, and I'll throw in a free tune-up!"

The salesman makes sense. You're not exactly going to climb the Rockies. The second model may be the right one for you. Some buyers will become flustered and say, "I'll take it!" But you stand back and say, "Okay, thanks. Let me check out that same bike at the other bicycle store." After all, the second model is probably even less expensive at the first store than the second store.

That's how you should react when a mortgage company tries to switch loan programs on you. If in fact you do change your mind from a 20-year fixed-rate loan to a 7/1 hybrid, it's important to call the other lenders for a quote on the same program. Otherwise you could get snookered into the wrong loan.

Get Quotes at the Same Time of Day

Don't bother getting interest rate quotes early in the morning, unless you're on the West Coast. Lenders don't price their mortgage rates until they've had time to digest all the daily economic reports that are released mid-morning East Coast time. Most lenders set their rates no later than 11:00 A.M. EST, some a little later, some a little earlier.

Rates can move throughout the course of the day. If they move wildly enough—about $1/4$ of a point—lenders will "reprice" their loans—raising or lowering their rates and reissuing them.

Suppose you call two loan officers, speak directly with one, and leave a voice mail with the other. Later on in the afternoon, the loan officer for whom you left the message could call you back with a rate that's lower than the one you got from the first loan officer. It's possible that the mortgage markets were better in the afternoon and lenders adjusted their pricing. That's why you need to get your rate quotes at the same time of day.

Quoting with Points

This can be confusing and can muddy the rate waters if not approached correctly.

Points are sometimes called *discount points*, because paying points discounts the interest rate. One point typically reduces a 30-year fixed rate by $1/4$ percent. If 7.00 percent is available with no points, then your loan officer may also offer 6.75 percent with one point.

A point is 1 percent of the loan amount. It comprises 100 *basis points*. So, one point on a $250,000 loan is $2,500. One basis point is ¹/₁₀₀th of a percent of one point. Rates don't change much in basis points during the course of a trading day. It is rare for a rate to change by anything more than ¹/₄ percent during the day.

A loan officer will have a variety of available rate and point combinations to quote to her borrowers. A typical rate sheet would look something like the table here:

30-YEAR FIXED RATE

Rate	Point(s)
7.00%	0
6.875%	¹/₂
6.75%	1.00
6.625%	1¹/₂
6.50%	2

When getting interest rate quotes, it's important to make the rate comparison a constant in terms of points. The easiest comparison is a lender's rate for today with no points.

Validity

It's also important to get rate quotes that will apply long enough for you to close the deal. You can get rate quotes for up to six months or more, but the longer the time the rates are valid, the more you'll pay.

Lenders will issue rate quotes for as little as 7 or 15 days as well, but that wouldn't be enough time to get your loan package together and get approved. There are lots of things that happen during a loan approval. Even though you see advertisements such as "Same-Day Approval" or "Close Your Loan in a Week," it doesn't mean a whole lot unless all of the title work, appraisal, loan documentation, attorney review, and such has been completed.

Many contracts for existing condos, co-ops, and townhouses allow a 30-day period for buyers to close on their mortgage and take possession of the home. Thirty days is plenty of time to get all the things needed to close a mortgage loan.

If your loan closes in 45 days and you don't ask how long that rate will apply, it really doesn't matter what the rate is, because it probably won't be valid after 30 days.

If your loan closes in 45 days, you should get rate quotes from your different sources for just enough time necessary to close your deal. If you close in 45 days, don't accept a quote for 60 days. For each additional 15 days beyond a 30-day quote, you can expect to pay an additional $1/8$ of a point.

Origination Fees

Often quoted by mortgage brokers, an *origination fee* is also expressed as a percentage of the loan amount and is a fee to the mortgage company for producing, or originating, the loan for the lender. In some parts of the country, an origination fee is a standard charge and will be quoted on every rate offering as a matter of default.

If you're buying in an area where there's an origination fee, make sure all your loan officers include it in their quotes. A good question to ask would be, "What is your rate on a 30-year fixed-rate loan that is good for 30 days with no points and no origination charges?"

Aggregator Sites

Websites that list the rates of many mortgage companies are known as *aggregator sites*. These sites enable borrowers to make side-by-side rate comparisons.

Be wary of such sites, regardless of how professional they look or how long they've been in business. If you go to a popular aggregator site and look at 30-year fixed rates, for instance, you'll see maybe 20 or 30 lenders all touting their rates—and they'll be all over the map.

Some will quote rates with no points, some with one point, even some with 1.375 points. At the very least, it's confusing to the borrower. At worst, it's misleading. How can mortgage rates vary so much from one lender to another? In fact, they can't. That's because they price their loans on the same index. But they try and confuse buyers with various rate/point combinations.

You may want to use an aggregator site as a reference tool, but don't put too much stock in it. It's an advertisement. The rates may not be valid, even though today's date is right next to the rate. You'll find some rates that are legitimate and others that are not. You'll also see some very low interest rate quotes from mortgage companies that you've never heard of. Although their rate quotes can be enticing, to say the least, you can't determine whether the company—and more important, the loan officer you will be working with—is competent.

Another common type of website takes a loan application from you and then asks mortgage companies to "compete" against one another for your loan. Lending Tree pioneered this approach. It's certainly legitimate, but it's important to know there are other companies in existence that attempt to model the "bidding" process but in reality are only lead generators for loan officers.

Some loan officers don't develop and nurture relationships to drive their business. Instead, they pay for leads from a company that has names and contact information on people who want further information about mortgage loans.

It's no secret how lead-generation companies get their information: Some comes from public records, and some comes from potential borrowers who give their information to the lead companies.

When you're shopping for interest rates, you'll see various advertisements for companies that will take your basic information and then have mortgage companies call you directly. You fill out a form and submit your contact information, and then the lead company puts it in its database for sale to loan officers.

Oftentimes you'll be lured into giving your information based on an ultralow interest rate you saw advertised online. Even though you may know in your head that the rate being advertised is probably too good to be true, you decide, "Aw, what the heck, it's worth a shot!" Soon you'll be contacted by mortgage companies you've never heard of.

The simple fact remains that you have not applied for any mortgage so far, and the mortgage companies that contact you have no idea whatsoever of the advertised rate you saw. They only know that you may be interested in a mortgage.

I recall filling out one of those online forms for that very reason—because I saw an ultralow rate advertised. I didn't actually want a mortgage, but I did want to watch the mechanism to see what would happen after I filled out the lead generator's online form.

After a couple of days (which surprised me because I thought I would have been contacted sooner), I got one call from a woman who said she was referred to me and asked what I was looking for.

I told her that I had already indicated that on the form I had filled out after seeing the ultralow rate. She said she didn't have that information and repeated her request: "What type of loan are you looking for?" I said I wanted a refinance at the 3 percent rate advertised. She said that she didn't have anything that was 3 percent and wasn't aware of any rate being advertised by the lead company. I told her that it was advertised, and then I waited on the phone while she went to the very same website I did. That's when she saw the low rate.

She told me she was sorry that she couldn't get that rate but did have some very competitive programs and would I mind if she reviewed them with me? I told her I did mind and hung up the phone.

There is no reason to use an online company to get your financing. You'll be working with people you've never heard of (and whom you're likely never to hear from again). Such mortgage companies close a loan, then go back to the pile of leads they bought from a lead generator.

On the other hand, a loan officer who is local and who has been referred to you will do whatever it takes to keep her reputation intact. Loan officers get paid only when they close a deal. If they gain a reputation of screwing up deals, they'll find themselves out of work because no one will send business their way.

When using an online company, what do loan officers bring to the game? Do they care about getting more business from you in the future? Do they want you to refer them to your friends and neighbors? Do they have a relationship with your Realtor?

If you went to your closing table and found that the interest rate you'd been quoted was not on your loan papers or that previously undisclosed closing costs had magically appeared, do you think a local loan officer who had been referred to you and was thoroughly vetted would have misquoted you in the first place or done whatever it took to get things right? Of course, if you did your homework that's exactly what would have happened.

An online lender may not care about the long term, only the now. And if online lenders mess up your loan, they simply go back to the pile and grab another lead.

FACTORS THAT CAN AFFECT YOUR RATE QUOTE

When you're shopping for rates, there are certain assumptions that can affect the quote—and many consumers are unaware of that. It's your loan officer's job, however, to ask certain questions to give you an accurate rate quote. And unless every one of the mortgage companies makes an apples-to-apples quote, you're going to have skewed quotes. Factors that can affect your quote are: credit score, down payment versus sales price, subordinate financing, and occupancy.

Credit Score

Higher or lower credit scores can impact a rate quote and can adjust when evaluating the other three quote factors at the same time.

We'll discuss scores and how they work in more detail in chapter 5, but essentially the worse the credit the higher the rate.

When you call around to different lenders for rate quotes, they're going to assume you have good credit. Typically, any score above 700 will get you the best rates. But when scores begin to fall below that number, rates can begin to rise and finally disqualify you altogether.

Most people have a pretty good idea of whether they have good credit. If you pay your bills on time, your credit is probably just fine.

Down Payment Versus Sales Price

In general, the bigger your down payment, the better your rate will be; and the less you put down, the higher your rate.

Most rate quotes assume 20 percent down, but if you only have 5 percent down your rate can be higher. It could be higher still if you have 5 percent down and a 675 credit score.

Your loan officer is supposed to ask you not only how much you want to borrow, but also the sale price or current value of the property so she can give you an accurate quote. If you are able to put down more money (up to 25 percent down), you may get a lower rate. Be sure to ask your loan officer about this.

Subordinate Financing

Subordinate financing means there is another loan on the property (or will be) when you close on the purchase of your condo.

Some buyers put only 5 percent down—and they get a higher rate than those who put 20 percent down. What's more, loans with less than 20 percent down require a *mortgage insurance* policy, which adds to the monthly payment. We'll look at mortgage insurance in detail in chapter 4.

To avoid mortgage insurance, a buyer can take out one loan at 80 percent of the sale price, and a second loan that is the difference between the down payment, the first mortgage, and the price of the condo. For example, on a $250,000 property the first mortgage would be 80 percent of that, or $200,000—avoiding mortgage insurance. The down payment would be 10 percent, or $25,000, and finally the subordinated note would be at $25,000 as well. Loans with subordinate financing may have a higher rate than those without subordinate financing.

These rate adjustments can be slight—an adjustment in the amount of discount points you pay. It may increase your rate as well. The chart on page 75 shows the various combinations of score, loan, and subordinate financing.

This chart shows that a credit score of anything greater than 720 has no adjustments regardless of how much is put down. The <=60 percent is the loan amount compared to the value of the property. It means any loan less than 60 percent of the value of the property, for instance.

But look at credit scores between 680 and 699. Now move across to the loan-to-value column that is >85 percent. You can see that there is an increase in price by 0.500, which is $1/2$ of a discount point.

This translates into an approximate increase in the mortgage rate by either $1/2$ point or $1/8$ percent in rate. The chart is a tad complicated for the consumer but is read every day by loan officers who quote rates.

Or at least they're supposed to read it. You can see how complicated a simple rate quote may be, but most mortgage programs have certain adjustments based on a variety of factors.

It's also important to note that although lenders' adjustments can be different from one company to another, there is no universal chart. They can be similar, but not exactly alike for all lenders.

Occupancy

The final adjustment for a rate quote has to do with occupancy. Do you intend to occupy the property as your primary residence?

Conventional Fixed-Price Adjustments Score vs. Loan to Value

Credit Score	<= 60%	>60-<=70%	>70-<=75%	>75-<=80%	>80-<=85%	>85-<=90%	>90-<=95%	>95-<=97%
>= 740	0.000	0.000	0.000	0.000	0.000	0.000	0.000	0.000
720 – 739	0.000	0.000	0.000	0.000	0.000	0.000	0.000	0.000
700 – 719	0.000	0.500	0.500	0.500	0.500	0.500	0.500	0.500
680 – 699	0.000	0.500	0.500	0.500	0.500	0.500	0.500	0.500
660 – 679	0.000	0.500	1.250	1.250	1.250	1.250	1.250	n/a
640 – 659	0.000	0.500	1.750	1.750	1.750	1.750	1.750	n/a
620 – 639	0.000	0.750	2.500	2.500	2.500	2.500	2.500	
< 620	0.000	0.750	2.750	2.750	2.750	2.750	2.750	

Cash Out Refinance Adjustments (in addition to adjustments above; does apply to 15-yr terms)

Credit Score	<= 60%	>60-<=70%	>70-<=75%	>75-<=80%	>80-<=85%	>85-<=90%	>90-<=95%	>95-<=97%
>= 740	0.000	0.000	0.000	0.250	0.375	0.375	n/a	n/a
720 – 739	0.000	0.125	0.000	0.125	0.500	0.500	n/a	n/a
700 – 719	0.000	0.125	0.750	0.250	0.750	1.500	n/a	n/a
680 – 699	0.000	0.250	0.750	2.000	0.750	2.000	n/a	n/a
660 – 679	0.000	0.250	2.000	1.750	2.500	3.000	n/a	n/a
640 – 659	0.000	0.750	n/a	n/a	n/a	n/a	n/a	n/a
620 – 639	0.000	0.750	n/a	n/a	n/a	n/a	n/a	n/a
< 620	1.000	1.750	n/a	n/a	n/a	n/a	n/a	n/a

Occupancy is one of the more important adjustments to rate that lenders make. If you don't intend to live in the property, the interest rate can be anywhere from $1/4$ to $3/8$ percent higher than if you do intend to live there.

Lenders evaluate several risk factors when issuing a mortgage. Someone renting the property out poses a greater risk of default than someone living there. After all, if someone owns a primary residence and a rental and loses his job, which property do you think would be more likely to go into *foreclosure* or be sold? That's right, the rental. Lenders adjust for that risk.

There is a third occupancy factor: a "second" or "vacation" home. A second home is simply another property where you live for part of the year. Think of someone who lives in Minnesota from the spring through the fall, then moves to Phoenix for the winter.

If you're buying a second home, the lender will determine whether the "vacation" home moniker would apply. Because vacation homes won't carry as high a rate premium as rentals, buyers may be tempted to lie on the loan application about the status of the property in question.

If you live in Minnesota and you're buying a unit in Phoenix, then a lender would be convinced it is in fact a second home. If you live in Minnesota and are buying in Minnesota, then you're going to have to make a pretty good case about the status of your potential purchase, especially so if your new unit is in the same town.

HOW TO CHANGE MORTGAGE COMPANIES MIDSTREAM

Okay, you did all your homework, interviewed your loan officers, and made your choice. Then you found out that despite all your effort and the best intentions, you made a mistake and went with the wrong loan officer.

Maybe the rate was quoted incorrectly. Perhaps the loan officer is being rude to you. Or your intuition tells you something is not right. Can you simply switch? Yes, but there are certain things you need to consider first.

The very first consideration is how far along you are in the loan process. If your property is scheduled to close in five days, you don't have time to switch. But if you're only a few days into your *escrow* period, it could be a good idea to call another lender that you didn't initially choose.

Next, before you switch lenders, call the other lender to see if it can still offer the same loan program it originally quoted to you. Or better yet, have rates dropped since you last spoke?

If you decide to leave one lender and go with another, you should contact the lender you're leaving and officially cancel the application.

There will be different cancellation procedures from one lender or mortgage broker to the next, but many do ask for a written cancellation. You can send that cancellation in an e-mail or perhaps there's a form you need to sign. Just be sure you let the other lender know you're leaving it, and why. If the lender made some errors, it will want to fix things and make it up to you instead of losing a loan altogether.

Remember that loan companies don't get paid until a loan closes, and there is no small amount of work that a mortgage company puts into a loan application just to get it to the closing table. If that loan never closes, the mortgage company loses money.

But hey, forget about them, right? They're the ones who made you mad, so you're switching. But the lender can't transfer your loan package—which includes your initial loan application, pay stubs, bank statements, and all the documentation required to get your loan approved—to another lender. Instead, you'll have to complete a brand-new loan application with the new lender. They'll have to document the file all over again. The lender will contact the attorney and title company to get the legal documents to reflect the new lender's information. The appraisal will have to be changed to have the new lender's name on it. And sometimes a brand-new appraisal will have to be performed.

Some lenders ask for appraisal money up front when you apply for a mortgage loan. Others do not. An interesting fact of paying for appraisals is that even though you pay for the appraisal, typically about $350.00 or so, the appraisal belongs to the lender. You'll get a copy of the appraisal, but on the front of the appraisal it will say something to the effect of, "Prepared for XYZ Mortgage Company."

You can transfer an appraisal, but the appraiser will demand that the appraisal be paid for if it hasn't been already. Also, be prepared to pay a $50 to $100 "retype" fee to include the new lender's information in the appraisal documents.

We'll discuss closing costs in more detail in chapter 7, but be wary of how some lenders ask for money up front to pay for appraisals. Some lenders simply ask for a check to be made out to the lender for $350 for an appraisal, whereas others ask for a $350 application fee. What's the difference?

If you paid an application fee and not an appraisal fee, then when you try to transfer the appraisal to your new lender, you just may find out that the appraiser has not yet been paid for his work, even though you paid $350. In fact, you may have to pay another $350 for an appraisal. After all, you paid an application fee, not an appraisal fee.

This may sound a tad unethical, and maybe it is. Just be clear when you make out a check to the lender that it's going to pay for the appraisal. To help establish this fact, on the "memo" line on your check write "money for appraisal."

If you get into a shoving match with your lender, you can point out that the check was for an appraisal, regardless of what the lender says. It's hard to imagine a lender not cooperating, but I have seen loan officers hold appraisals hostage.

HOW TO LOCK IN THE MORTGAGE RATE

In the previous sections, we discussed how to find the best loan officer and mortgage rate. But unless that mortgage rate is guaranteed or "locked in," it may not be good.

When you lock in an interest rate, you're guaranteeing that the rate will be reserved for you when you go to the closing table. If you're not locked in, then you'll be subject to market conditions and you'll take whatever's available when the lender gets ready to print out your closing papers.

If you've done all the hard work of finding the best deal, don't mess up by not locking in that rate.

Lenders take locks very seriously—just as seriously as you do. If you lock in a rate with a lender, the lender reserves that rate for you. If you go to another lender, it will have to replace your lock with someone else's loan, or else it could pay a premium for taking out money and not using it.

Lenders don't lock you automatically. If you call and get a rate quote the lender isn't going to reserve that money and that rate for you without your express permission. You have to tell your loan officer you want to lock in your rate. What are the procedures for locking in?

Mortgage companies can have different internal guidelines and paperwork for you to fill out. But at minimum, the lender will ask that you complete a loan application with it before it locks. A lender won't lock you over the phone without a loan application; this keeps people from calling up lenders on the phone and verbally locking in a mortgage rate while still shopping around for other lenders.

Some lenders will ask you to pay for your appraisal ahead of time when you apply with them. This means you must have a condo, co-op, or townhouse already picked out, and that you've got a sales contract in your hand.

What if you lock in and then the rates go down? Then you get whatever you locked in at. Rate locks protect both the borrower and the lender. When you lock in at 6 percent and rates go up, you're protected. If you lock in at 6 percent and rates go down, then you still get the rate you locked in.

Get your lock agreement in writing. Don't make a verbal

agreement; there will be no record of your lock request. Until you get written confirmation that your rate is indeed locked in for the amount of time you need, don't feel as though you've got your rate guaranteed.

There are no specific lending laws that determine how a rate-lock agreement should read or what it should look like. But all national lenders, retail banks, and larger mortgage bankers have a form. If you're working with a mortgage broker, it's likely they'll have their own form as well. If they don't, the wholesale lender will have one.

Why not trust a verbal agreement? Besides the obvious reason previously mentioned, it's also possible that the loan officer didn't get around to locking you in. She might have forgotten, but more likely she could be trying to make a little extra money. Here's how it works: Say you call your loan officer and tell her, "Okay, lock me in at 7 percent," and the loan officer says, "There. You're locked." Sounds pretty straightforward, right? But sometimes a loan officer will gamble that rates will drop slightly. If they do, the loan officer can then lock you in at the rate you requested and make, say, another $1/4$ point on the loan.

Most major banks and mortgage bankers have strict guidelines against floating a lock so the loan officer can exploit *market gains*. For starters, it's unethical because it's not what the buyer and the loan officer agreed to. Also, it's possible for the loan officer to make a "bad bet" on the market and lose *your* money. So, to avoid having to start over again (not to mention the possibility of suing the lender), when it comes to locking in a rate, get it in writing.

Mortgage brokers have become more regulated and whole-sale lenders are requiring that if there are any market gains the mortgage broker must have you sign a piece of paper acknowledging that she is making more on the loan than you had previously thought. We'll discuss such disclosure in chapter 6.

Mortgage brokers, because they're set up with multiple wholesale lenders, may also lock you in at one bank and then, if rates go down, simply lock you in at another lender at the new, lower rate. This can happen on occasion, but wholesale lenders also monitor what is called a "pull-through" rate, which shows the number of loans locked with the wholesale lender compared to the number of those locked loans that were actually delivered. When a wholesale lender sees, for example, that a broker locks in loans, then delivers only 25 percent of them, pretty soon that broker will no longer be allowed to work with the wholesale lender.

If, while shopping for a lender, a loan officer tells you that because they're a mortgage broker, if rates go down they'll simply send you to another lender, be aware of one thing: If the broker regularly engages in this practice, soon they won't have anyone to send loans to because their pull-through rate will be so low.

Some loans offer a free *float-down* feature that allows you to renegotiate your interest rate if rates fall precipitously during your contract period. Few lenders offer an official float down, but typically the interest rate must have been reduced by more than $1/8$ percent and the broker pays a $1/2$ to $3/8$ percent float-down fee.

You'll need to ask up front if the loan has a float-down feature. Float downs aren't free, but when rates drop enough, they may be a good option.

The final way to get the lower rate if rates have moved down after you locked in is simply to ask the lender to honor the new, lower rates. Loan officers can be very well aware that if the new lower rates aren't honored, you could walk away from the deal and go elsewhere, given enough time to transfer your loan and close on time.

That being said, if you demand that your lender, "Reduce your interest rate, or else!" when you're five days away from your closing, the lender won't honor your request. That's because he knows that you run the risk of not closing on time and losing your earnest money deposit, and perhaps the property.

DEBT RATIOS AND HOW LENDERS CALCULATE THEM

You may have heard the term *debt ratio*. Debt ratio plays a critical role in how much a lender will loan you. You can shop all you want for interest rates, but what that rate ultimately represents is your monthly payment. And lenders have a formula that helps determine whether you can afford your payments. That formula is the debt ratio.

A debt ratio comes in two types: a *housing ratio* and a *total debt ratio*—sometimes called a *front and back ratio*.

A lender will take your total monthly house payment,

including principal, interest, taxes, and HOA fees, and divide that number by your gross monthly income.

For instance, let's say your principal and interest payment is $1,000, taxes are $100, and HOA dues are $75, which adds up to $1,175. Now imagine your gross income each month is $4,000. Divide $1,175 by $4,000 and the answer is 0.294, or 29.4 percent. Your housing, or front, ratio is 29.4.

Now take that same $1,175 and add your car payment of $350 and a student loan payment of $100, and you get $1,625. Dividing that number by $4,000 gives you 0.406, or 40.6 percent. Your total or back debt ratio is 40.6.

Your debt ratios in this example would be $29.4/40.6$. What is the maximum debt ratio a lender can allow?

Although there are no maximum limits, the historical standard was around $28/36$. But over the years, loan approvals have begun to take a more holistic approach. Today they look at the borrower's overall picture and tend not to decline someone due to just one aspect of the debt ratio.

Again, in this example you wouldn't be declined because your back ratio was 40.6 and not 36. But lenders do start to get a little nervous when ratios exceed 45. It's not a deal killer, especially if there are other factors that compensate for the higher ratio, such as excellent credit or a down payment of 10 percent or more.

| CHAPTER 4 |

Specialty Loans, Government Programs, and Refinance Loans

MORTGAGE LOANS CAN BE USED for purposes other than buying a property. The following list comprises different types of mortgage loans: interest only, equity, no money down, government bond programs, and portfolio.

INTEREST ONLY

We touched on an *interest-only* loan feature when discussing payment-option ARMs. Sometimes an "interest-only" feature is added to a standard conventional fixed-rate mortgage.

It's easy enough to explain: You pay only the interest on the mortgage, not the principal. If you examine the first monthly payment on a 30-year fully amortized, fixed-rate mortgage on $250,000 at 6.50 percent, the payment would break down like this:

Principal and Interest Payment	$1,580.01
Amount to Principal	$ 226.00
Amount to Interest	$1,354.17

Now look 10 years down the road. You'll see that the principal is paid down; more of the monthly payment is now going toward principal, and less to interest.

Principal Balance	$211,940.32
Principal and Interest Payment	$ 1,580.01
Amount to Principal	$ 429.83
Amount to Principal	$ 1,150.34

A fully amortizing loan will have the loan paid off in exactly 30 years, but the interest-only feature allows that the borrower make only an interest payment. Most interest-only loans have the interest-only feature available for the first 10 years before turning into a 20-year fixed fully amortized loan.

Now look at the interest-only feature and again look 10 years down the road and the principal balance is $250,000.00.

The new monthly payment for a 20-year loan at 6.50 percent and $250,000 is $1,863.93 per month.

An interest-only feature can be added to a fixed-rate mortgage. The feature is designed to give monthly payment options to the buyers who may get paid a commission or earn large bonuses periodically. For those who opt for such a program, it's important not to get too comfortable with the interest-only feature. You do need to pay down the mortgage when you can (and these loans have no prepayment penalties).

Adding an interest-only feature typically increases the mortgage rate by $^1/_4$ percent compared to the same 30-year fixed rate mortgage without an interest-only feature.

EQUITY

An *equity loan* is a loan based on the equity in the property—or the difference between your loan and the value of your share in the case of a co-op. It's typically made after the original purchase loan was made, although that's certainly not a requirement. Your unit will have its equity comprised of what you originally put down plus appreciation (or minus depreciation).

A lender will then issue a loan based on that equity. The borrower can choose a home *equity line of credit* or one lump sum.

A lump sum payment is called an *equity loan* while a line of credit is called a *home equity line of credit*, or *HELOC*. Rates are typically based on the prime rate as its index and either adding or subtracting a margin, depending on the quality of the borrower and the amount of equity in the property when compared to the new equity loan.

Equity loans are calculated by using the *combined loan to value*, or CLTV. If the value of a property is $250,000 and the first mortgage has a $150,000 balance, the *loan to value*, or LTV, is 60 LTV. If there is a $50,000 equity line, the CLTV would be $150,000 plus the $50,000 equity line, or $200,000. That would represent an 80 percent CLTV.

100 percent CLTV equity loans will typically carry higher rates. Some lenders do not make 100 percent CLTV loans on condos, co-ops, or townhouses, but they will reduce the CLTV cap at 95 percent. That means a lender will require at least 5 percent equity in the property when issuing a home equity loan.

NO MONEY DOWN

Again, easy enough to understand. But a zero-money-down loan can come in the form of one big loan at 100 percent of the sale price; or it could be made up of two loans, such as an 80/20 loan where the first is at 80 percent LTV and the second, subordinated loan is at 20 percent LTV.

These loans are much harder to find today than in the past. The typical no-money-down loan is of the 80/20 variety. And a single loan is 100 percent of the value of the property; 100 percent loans will require mortgage insurance because the loan itself is greater than 80 percent of the sales price. Some mortgage insurance companies don't insure such loans, so the only choice would be a lender that has an arrangement with a mortgage insurance company to provide a *lender paid mortgage insurance*, or LPMI.

100 percent financing with LPMI is hardly an attractive rate as the mortgage insurance policy is actually paid for with a much higher rate. Unless you absolutely have to buy that perfect condo but at a time when you have very little cash to close, then a 100 percent loan might work for you. Sometimes in these situations it's best to wait and save some money for a

down payment; otherwise your payments will be higher when compared to a loan with a down payment.

No-money-down loans can cause problems when you have to sell the property. If you're planning to hold onto the unit for a long time, 100 percent financing may be okay. But if you're not sure how long you're going to keep the unit—or if you're forced to sell due to a job transfer or the loss of a job—you may not have enough equity in the property to cover the closing costs associated with selling.

This means that if you're forced to sell earlier than you planned, when you go to the closing table you will have to bring money. Zero equity in property, or even property that is "upside down" (the value of the property is less than what is owed on it), can cause real estate to go into foreclosure if the seller can't make the payments or bring enough funds to a closing.

GOVERNMENT BOND PROGRAMS

Sometimes simply called "Bond Money," these programs are typically dedicated to the first-time buyer and provide below-market rates from state- or city-sponsored bond programs.

Such programs typically require that the buyer take a homebuyer's education course and that the property be in a particular ZIP code or part of the city. There are other bond programs designed for teachers and public servants. Some states even offer additional mortgage rate incentives to qualified veterans.

These bond programs are used to lower the mortgage rate

on a conventional loan program and, depending upon the current market conditions, can be much lower than what is available. For instance, at one point, the Texas Veterans Land Board offered interest rates in the 4 percent range compared to conventional interest rates that were in the mid-6 percent range.

Bond programs are issued annually. Once the bond money is gone, buyers must wait until the next bond issuance before new funds become available.

PORTFOLIO

Although conventional and government loans are underwritten to exact standards established by Fannie Mae, Freddie Mac, FHA, and VA, sometimes the situation arises where either the borrower or the property doesn't quite fit the mold for any of these types of loans. What to do?

Get a *portfolio loan*—so named because the lender has no intentions of selling the loan, ever. Instead, the loan is kept in-house, or in the lender's "portfolio."

A common portfolio loan would be for someone who owns a lot of mortgaged real estate.

Co-ops will typically have a greater share of portfolio financing when compared to government or conventional financing simply because there are fewer portfolio lenders.

Or a lender would have a stern rule on someone being self-employed for a minimum of two years or that there is income that the buyer has but the lender won't recognize. Whatever the reason, a portfolio loan can be an alternative to traditional lending.

Portfolio loans aren't for people with poor credit—far from it. Banks can make a portfolio loan, but they have to be 100 percent convinced they're making the right decision. If a portfolio loan goes bad, it stays on the bank's books.

Portfolio loans are made to loyal bank customers who have a previous relationship with the buyer. The bank may have made a business loan to the buyer or the buyer keeps all his business and personal accounts with the bank. The bank knows the portfolio borrower by name.

Portfolio loans are relatively shorter in term—say three years or so—and are used simply as a short-term vehicle to acquire the property. The strategy is to get the condo with portfolio financing, then "fix" whatever is keeping the buyer from getting conventional financing during the term of the portfolio loan.

REFINANCING

A *refinance* is nothing more than replacing a current mortgage with a new one. It's pretty simple, but why would someone refinance a mortgage? Did they discover they got a bad loan and want to get out of it? Perhaps, but most refinances occurs when things have changed since the previous mortgage was placed.

Perhaps rates have dropped and you can save money each month. Or maybe you want to pull some cash out of your condo and pay off an automobile loan. A refinance is a good thing for people who originally got a loan when they had lower credit scores that gave them a higher rate, but who since have improved their credit. When they refinance, they get a lower rate.

There are plenty of reasons to refinance, but how do you know when and why you should ever consider refinancing a mortgage? As interest rates begin to drop, you'll begin to see advertisements in newspapers, hear them on the radio, and see them on the Internet trumpeting, "Rates dropped, refinance now!"

Perhaps you got a flyer in the mail from a mortgage company or your bank. However and whatever piques your interest, there are ways to determine whether a refinance is good for you. You shouldn't have to be talked into it by some aggressive loan officer.

A refinance pays off the old note(s) and replaces it with a new one. And it has a neat twist: It allows you to roll all your closing costs into your new mortgage, whereas when you first purchased the property you had to come up with your closing costs with extra funds.

Most refinances allow you to refinance up to 90 percent of the current appraised value of your property. FHA and VA loans will allow you to go up to 100 percent.

Let's look at the various reasons you may want to refinance: drop in rates, changing the term, pulling cash out, refinancing multiple loans, and ARM to fixed rate.

Dropping Rates

This is the most obvious reason to refinance. Say you got your original mortgage rate at 6.50 percent and rates have since dropped to 6.00 percent—and might move lower. As with any mortgage, there are closing costs involved. And you'll need a whole new round of fees similar to (and sometimes even more than) when you first bought the property. You'll need a new appraisal, a new *credit report*, a new title insurance policy, and more.

You may have heard or read somewhere that the way to know how to refinance is if rates drop 2 percent or more from your current rate. And, in fact, if rates did drop more than 2 percent it would be a good idea to refinance. But you probably shouldn't wait that long. In fact, rates haven't moved that much since mortgage rates hit a relative high in mid-2000, then dropped nearly 3 percent. Historically, however, at least over the past two decades we've seen rate moves typically within a 1 percent range over the course of one year. Up a little, down a little.

So is there a magic change in rate that works? Actually, no. Rates are a function of the loan amount and the term. You need to calculate the monthly payment and evaluate that first. Are rates and the payments essentially the same thing? Again, no. And here's why.

Calculate the payments on a 30-year 6.50 percent rate and a 7.00 percent rate on $500,000. You get $3,160 and $3,326 per month, respectively. Now do the same calculation, but on a $50,000 loan. The answer is $316 per month and $332 per month. Hold that thought for a moment.

We'll discuss closing costs for condos in detail in chapter 7, but say closing costs for a refinance add up to around $2,000.

When determining whether it's a good time to refinance, take the difference in monthly payments, not the difference in rate, and divide that into the closing costs. The result is the number of months it takes to "recover" those closing costs.

In this example, the difference in monthly payments on the $500,000 loan is $166 per month and on the $50,000 loan it's a $17 per month savings.

Divide the $166 savings into the $2,000 and the answer is 12.04, or 12 months to recover the closing costs needed to close the loan. Now divide the $17 monthly savings on the lower loan amount into the $2,000 worth of closing costs and the result is 117.6, or 118 months to recover the closing costs needed to close the transaction.

Do you see the difference? It's not the rate that's important; it's how long it takes to recover closing costs. So, pay little attention to the rate and a lot of attention to how much it will cost you to refinance and how long it will take to recover your costs.

There really is no ideal "recovery" period for closing costs as long as you keep the mortgage long enough to get the costs back. But 118 is way too long—that's nearly 10 years! But any recovery period within two to three years would be appropriate.

Rate locks and terms for refinances work exactly like rate locks and terms for purchases; it's the very same loan, just applied differently. That being said, how far should you allow rates to drop before you lock in?

In other words, if rates go down to 6 percent and your recovery period is 12 months, should you wait to squeeze out an additional $1/8$ percent or more? What if rates drop to 5.875 percent and you locked in at 6.00 percent?

I have seen this play out time and time again as I listened to my clients muse about how much further they thought rates would drop before they lock in.

Let's see how trying to squeeze out another $^1/_8$ percent gain can affect the refinance numbers.

Five years ago, when a buyer bought her property, she got a 7 percent 30-year mortgage on $300,000. The principal and interest payment on that note comes out to $1,995 per month. But now rates have come down dramatically over the past few months and she can get another 30-year fixed rate at 6.25 percent. Her new payment would be $1,842—a monthly savings of $153. She discusses the new rate with her loan officer and they determine together that it indeed is a good time to refinance.

But she wants to wait. She heard on the news that the Fed was likely to lower rates in the future and that the economy wasn't going to be out of the doldrums any time soon. In fact, many economists projected a recession. She thinks rates are going to dip further.

So she waited a couple of weeks and rates were still at 6.25 percent. Her loan officer encouraged her to lock in her rate and close the new deal, but she thought perhaps he was trying to get his commission check and had less regard for how rates might go lower.

She waited some more. And some more. In fact, three months went by while she was "playing the market" and waiting for rates to go down further. But she forgot to take into account that each month she waited she was throwing away money on the higher rate. After three months had passed, she lost $459 in savings, trying to get the rate to move down just a tad more.

While she was concentrating on the interest rate, she didn't consider what the rate actually represented: her mortgage payment. She would have locked in an interest rate at 6 $^1/_8$ percent if it became available, but rates were stubbornly in the 6.25 percent range.

A difference in $^1/_8$ percent results in a drop in payment by only about $20 per month on her loan. If she divided that $20 into the $459 she "lost," she would find out that by waiting three months to save $20 per month it would take 22.9 months to recover lost interest.

Her loan officer told her that the monthly payment wouldn't go down much more and that she'd already saved $153 by refinancing from the 7 percent rate. She said she'd think about it and would call him back the next day.

She did sleep on it, thinking how much mental stress she was causing herself wondering what rates were going to do, and if her magical 6 $^1/_8$ percent rate would be available the next day.

The next day she did indeed call her loan officer and asked him to lock her in at 6 $^1/_4$ percent. But he couldn't. That morning, an unemployment report was released by the government showing that many more people were back at work than had been estimated, and that the economy was growing instead of heading toward a recession.

That immediately translated into higher mortgage rates, causing the 6 $^1/_4$ percent rate to move up to 6 $^1/_2$ percent that very morning. Now she had to decide if she should wait to see if rates would go back down to 6 $^1/_4$ percent, the rate she could have gotten a few months earlier.

She decided she didn't want to go through all of that again

and refinanced at $6^{1}/_{2}$ percent, dropping her payment to $1,896. Still a good deal, just not as good as she could have gotten.

Changing the Term

Another popular reason to refinance is to change the loan term, or amortization period. Perhaps the most common term refinance is for a shorter term on the note to reduce the amount of long-term interest that's being paid.

Look at the amount of interest paid on a 30-, 25-, 20-, 15-, and 10-year loan amount of $300,000:

Term	Rate	Interest Paid
30 year	6.50%	$382,560
25 year	6.50%	$307,500
20 year	6.50%	$236,640
15 year	6.25%	$162,960
10 year	6.25%	$104,160

As you can easily tell from the chart, the longer the term the more interest you pay. Perhaps a buyer first got a 30-year fixed rate mortgage when he or she bought a condo but now feels more comfortable making higher payments to reduce the term and the amount of interest paid by refinancing to shorter term.

Depending on how far rates actually fall during a potential refinance period, one could also reduce the term of the loan while keeping the payments about the same as they originally were. How does that work?

Let's say that someone bought his condo when rates were at relative highs, say 7.25 percent. On a $300,000 loan, that works out to $2,046 per month. A few short years later rates begin to fall, with 20-year rates dropping to about 5 $^{1}/_{2}$ percent.

Refinance that same $300,000 into a 20-year loan, and the monthly payment works out to $2,063 per month. Now compare that with a 30-year loan at 5.50 percent. Although the payment is lower at $1,703 per month, the amount of interest on the 20- and the 30-year loans would be:

30 year	$313,080
20 year	$195,120

Yes, the borrower could have reduced his payment by a considerable amount, but the long-term interest is staggering. The borrower was comfortable making the original $2,046 per month payment. By keeping the payment yet refinancing the term, he accomplished his goal of eliminating a significant chunk of interest that would have been paid to the lender.

Another common refinance occurs when anticipating a life event, such as retirement or college plans.

A couple who wished to retire mortgage-payment-free in 15 years could refinance into a 15-year loan and watch the loan disappear right around their retirement age.

I recall a client who saw me for a refinance and had a similar life event on the horizon. In fact, he refinanced from a 15-year to a 10-year. This resulted in a relatively significant jump in his monthly payment. Rates had dropped, but not by enough to offset the increase in mortgage payment. But he had a plan.

He knew he could afford to make extra payments each month to pay off this mortgage, but he also said he "knew himself enough" that unless the monthly payment was made automatically he might not have the discipline to make those regular payments.

In this case, he had a daughter who would be college age in 10 years, and he didn't want to be saddled with college costs and a mortgage at the same time. By knocking five years off his mortgage, he knew not only that his home would be free and clear during a tested cash-flow time in his life, but that he would be able to afford to send his daughter to pretty much any college.

Another reason people refinance is to lengthen the loan term. Lengthening the term reduces the monthly payment while adding long-term interest. Sometimes things happen and it becomes necessary to reduce the monthly payment regardless of the increased interest.

Often this type of refinance is associated with a divorce situation where one spouse wants to keep the house but may not be able to afford payments on a 15-year loan.

Or perhaps someone retires or loses his or her job. The former dual-income family is now a one-income family—and will likely remain so for some time, possibly for the remainder of the loan term.

A $300,000 15-year loan at 6.25 percent comes to monthly payments of $2,572. This requires approximately $9,000 per month in income to qualify for a mortgage loan. By refinancing that $300,000 into a 30-year loan at 6.50 percent, the payment drops to $1,896 and the qualifying monthly income is reduced by $2,200 to around $6,800.

Pulling Cash Out

A "cash-out" refinance can change the rate and/or the term but instead of simply paying off the old mortgage, you walk away with some extra cash that was pulled from your equity. Most *cash-out* refinances allow you to refinance up to 75 percent of the value of the condo and even up to 80 percent of the value if you pay a $1/4$ percent higher. The higher LTV option at 80 percent rarely works out when you consider the additional funds that are combined with the higher interest.

Let's look at a cash-out example at 75 percent and 80 percent, with a $200,000 value and a current loan balance of $100,000. We'll leave out closing costs in this example to keep the math a little easier.

At 75 percent LTV, the loan amount would be $150,000; and at 6.25 percent the payment would be $948. Subtract the $100,000 old loan, and the net is $50,000.

At 80 percent LTV the loan amount would be $160,000, and the payment would be $1,011 per month with the higher loan and higher rate. The net is $10,000 more, but your monthly payments are $63 higher. That yields another $22,600 or so in additional long-term interest.

Cash-out refinances can be good, but they must be executed with eyes wide open. If you just need some extra cash for home improvements or to pay off a car note, get an equity line instead. Equity lines have little or no closing costs. If all you want is $50,000, then consider an equity line instead of refinancing with all the associated costs. Only do a cash-out refinance if you're going to refinance anyway, due to rate or term.

Loan officers get trained to scour through old loan applications or make slick mailers touting the advantages of a cash-out refinance. They may look at one of your old loan applications, see that you had a car loan and some credit card debt, and send you a note saying you could save lots of money with a cash-out refinance. You'll rarely get a sales pitch from loan officers wanting to place an equity line with you because they don't get paid much, if anything, on an equity line.

The phone call might go something like, "Hey Dave, just checking in on you. Say, I was reviewing some old files and saw that you have a couple of car payments that add up to about $1,200. You know, we could refinance your current loan and although your rate won't go down a whole lot, we could pay off those cars and it'd save you a bundle, not to mention that now the interest on the car loans would be tax deductible because the loan is mortgage interest and not a consumer loan!"

The loan officer has already run the numbers before he calls you and yes, he's right: Your total monthly payments would drop. Here's the scenario:

Current mortgage balance	$200,000
Current rate	6.75%
Current payment	$1,297
Current car balances	$59,000
Current rate	10.00%
Current car payments	$1,200
House and car payments	$2,497
New mortgage balance	$259,000
New rate	6.375%
New payment	$1,615

You just traded a $2,497 payment in for a $1,615 payment. Common sense (and plain arithmetic) tells you that you saved $882, right? At first glance it appears so. But the difference between an auto loan and a 30-year mortgage is about 25 years. Yes, your payment dropped, but the auto payments would have gone away after less than five years.

In less than five years you would still own the car, but you would no longer have to pay the automobile loan. Today your monthly payments are $318 higher while you make the car payments. Say you consolidate and pay off the car loan today. How long before you sell or trade for a new car—and take on a whole new set of auto loan payments?

Cash-out refinances are not bad things. But you need to be fully aware of both the short- and the long-term effects of pulling out additional cash.

Another cash-out "pitch" is to refinance the loan, pull as much cash out as you can, and then invest the difference in stocks or bonds—or perhaps entrust those funds to an investment adviser your loan officer happens to know (and exchanges leads with).

When you are solicited to pull out cash it's usually in the loan officer's interest, not in yours. Those sales pitches and marketing gimmicks can be pretty convincing, so beware.

Refinancing Multiple Loans

Refinancing more than a mortgage can be a good idea because rates for the subordinated loans will always be higher than the mortgage. Say you buy a townhouse at 10 percent down. To avoid paying mortgage insurance you gets two loans, the first at 80 percent of the value of the property and the second at 10 percent of the value—an $80/10/10$ loan.

A typical scenario would be:

Sales Price	$200,000
Down Payment	$20,000

First Mortgage	$160,000 at 6.50%, 30 years, and $1,011 per month
Second Mortgage	$20,000 at 7.50%, 20 years, and $161 per month

Three years later, the economy begins to slow and mortgage rates start to fall with a 30-year mortgage rate dropping all the way down to 5.50 percent. You see that you can now combine the two notes into one 30-year loan. And because the value of the townhouse has gone up to $225,000, you can not only refinance to lower rates, but also avoid mortgage insurance because your loan will be at 80 percent of the new appraised value. Now it looks like this:

New First Mortgage	$180,000 at 5.50 percent, 30 years, and $1,022 per month

That's a savings of $150 per month. By dividing that into the closing costs of $2,500, the recovery period is $2,500 / $150 = 16.7 months, well within acceptable recovery range.

One can also refinance an old first mortgage with an adjustable home equity line.

ARM to Fixed Rate

When rates are at relative highs, some people elect to choose an ARM or a hybrid for the lower initial rates. But when rates fall, it's a good idea to consider getting out of an ARM or a hybrid and lock in rates for the long term when they're at relative lows. This is especially true if you plan to keep the property long term. If you're not keeping the property long term and expect to sell or otherwise dispose of it, then keep your ARM or hybrid.

This is something that should be considered well before a hybrid's reset date. For instance, you have a 5/1 hybrid at 5 percent and current 30-year fixed rates are at 6 percent. Should you wait until just before the hybrid resets and then refinance? Maybe not. Although there may be general rate trends, there is no way to predict what interest rates will be in the future.

So, the prudent approach would be to go ahead and refinance out of the hybrid and into a fixed rate if you're satisfied with the current rate.

GOVERNMENT PROGRAMS FOR CONDOS AND TOWNHOUSES

Both the state and federal governments have special loan programs to help purchase a condo or townhouse. These programs range from outright mortgages to down payment assistance programs aiding those who are having trouble finding money to close on a property.

Some of these programs require that the buyer be a first-time homebuyer or make a certain amount of money, while others have no requirements whatsoever. Either way, it makes sense to explore any available government programs that can help.

Conventional mortgages that are backed by Fannie Mae and Freddie Mac aren't direct loans. Fannie and Freddie don't make mortgage loans; they just buy them from lenders. It's the lender that's on the hook if the mortgage loan goes bad. With government loans, if the loan goes bad the government will guarantee a certain portion of it. There are two types of government-backed mortgages: VA and FHA loans.

VA Loans

Backed by the Department of Veterans Affairs, VA loans are hands-down the best option for those who qualify. VA loans require zero money down while offering interest rates just as competitive as those issued for conventional loans.

Historically, VA loans could only be placed on owner-occupied single-family residences, townhouses, and condominiums— but not cooperatives. Recently, legislation was signed that allowed for VA financing to be made available to those wishing to buy a co-op in New York City. Other cities may soon follow suit.

But VA loans aren't available for everyone. In fact, they're only for people who have served in the armed forces.

In 1944, Congress enacted the GI Bill, giving those who served in World War II various *entitlements* as a "thank you" for serving their country. Education benefits, pensions, and medical and housing assistance were provided for qualifying veterans.

Today, there are around 25 million who qualify for a VA loan and those people include those who served in the armed forces, active-duty personnel who have served at least 181 days, those who are in the National Guard or Reserve, and spouses of deceased veterans who died as a result of service-related injuries.

If you fall into one of these categories, you should explore the VA loan first. You'll need to obtain a *certificate of eligibility* from the federal government.

Conventional loans require that you make a down payment of at least 5 percent. And remember, if your first mortgage is more than 80 percent of the sale price you'll need mortgage insurance.

VA loans require no down payment and no mortgage insurance. They do, however, have a requirement for a VA *funding fee*—about 2.15 percent of the loan amount. It is this fee that the VA uses to provide funds to lenders when borrowers default; it is a requirement on every VA loan.

However, the funding fee may be rolled into the loan and not be paid out of pocket. In fact, every VA loan I've ever done had the funding fee rolled into the loan.

Let's compare a VA loan with a conventional one with minimum down payments for each.

SALES PRICE $300,000

	Loan Amount	Payment at 6.50%	Down
VA Loan	$306,360	$1,936	0
Conventional	$285,000	$1,986 (incl. MI)	$15,000

You can see that even when the funding fee is included in the loan amount, the total monthly payment is still less than a conventional loan that requires a mortgage insurance policy. You also save $15,000 in down payment funds, which can be used for other things such as closing costs, remodeling, savings, or investing.

Beyond their eligibility requirements, VA loans have no special requirements or limits compared to conventional loans. In fact, there are even provisions for using VA financing when the sale price is above the conforming limit. This is known as the "VA Jumbo."

For years, the Veterans Administration has allowed VA *Jumbo loans*. But hardly anyone knows about them. The current VA loan limit with zero down is $417,000, matching the *conforming loan* limits set by Fannie Mae and Freddie Mac. But the VA does make allowances for VA loans above that amount—way above. Say around $700,000.

Jumbo fixed rates can be anywhere from 1.00 percent to 1.50 percent higher than conforming rates. That's a lot, and it has many Jumbo buyers in a quandary. A 30-year fixed conforming rate might be 6.00 percent while a similar Jumbo rate could be 7.50 percent. It did not used to be so vast a spread. Prior to the recent mortgage mess, Jumbo rates were typically about $1/4$ to $1/2$ percent higher than a conforming loan. But not so with a VA Jumbo loan. VA Jumbo rates are about a $1/4$ percent higher than conforming rates. And loans can be as high as $700,000. So how does this work?

First, if you're a qualified veteran or reservist in search of a no-money-down loan, there simply is no better home loan out there. Even when every lender on the planet was shouting, "No Money Down!" for their home loans, they couldn't hold a candle to a VA loan when comparing rates and closing costs—as long as the VA loan didn't exceed $417,000 ($625,000 for Alaska and Hawaii).

But a little "quirk" in VA lending allows for VA loans above $417,000 as long as the veteran comes up with some down payment—same as with any Jumbo mortgage.

To figure out how much down payment a veteran will need, simply multiply the amount of the sales price over $417,000 and take 25 percent of that. For instance, a home sells for $650,000. Now subtract the maximum zero-down VA loan amount of $417,000 and you get $233,000. Twenty-five percent of $233,000 is $58,250. That's the down payment needed from the veteran.

That works out to about 9 percent down payment on a $650,000 home! As on all VA loans, there is a funding fee of about 2.2 percent of the loan amount. But that can be rolled into the loan and not paid out of pocket. In this example, the final loan amount would be about $604,750.

With a conventional Jumbo loan, you'd need 20 percent down and pay a higher rate, say 7.50 percent compared to 6.25 percent.

Not all lenders will offer this program, so you'll need to do a little homework. And even those who do offer it may have their own VA Jumbo limits. But if you're in the Jumbo market and are VA eligible, then you need to explore this option because most Jumbo loans will require a larger down payment along with the higher rates.

VA loans also restrict certain closing costs, further protecting the veteran. We'll discuss closing costs in detail in chapter 7, but the only fees that are allowable for the veteran to pay are those for:

Appraisal

Credit

Title and title-related fees

Origination fees or discount points

Recording fees

An easy way to remember which charges the veteran may pay is to simply remember the acronym ACTOR.

Sometimes, however, this restricted closing-cost benefit can be a hindrance. For instance, there might be a lender's loan-processing fee or a document-preparation fee. The veteran does not pay these fees. So who does? Either the lender or the seller.

But sometimes—especially when closing costs that can't be charged to the veteran add up to $1,000 or so—sellers might not be inclined to pay those fees and they'll reject your offer.

Typically, your Realtor will negotiate to get the seller to pay those charges. Many contracts are made with the seller offering to pay certain closing costs; a contract can be written specifying that the seller pay the veteran's "nonallowable" closing charges as part of the deal.

What if the seller is not willing to pay? If the real estate market is doing well the seller may simply decline your offer. If that's the case, you may consider changing your offer to reflect the amount of closing costs you're willing to pay.

For example, say your nonallowable closing charges add up to $1,500. You offer $200,000 and are rejected because of the additional closing costs that the seller does not want to pay. You could simply increase your offer to $201,500. Yes, your loan amount will go up slightly, but now the seller can pay those additional costs while still netting the same amount.

Some veterans believe that because they are eligible for the VA program they will automatically qualify for a loan. That is not the case. You still need to qualify for the loan in terms of credit and income. If there are credit issues or your debt ratios are too high, then you may not qualify for the loan—and your certificate of eligibility won't matter.

FHA Loans

Another type of government-backed mortgage is the *FHA loan*. Congress created the Federal Housing Administration, or FHA, in 1934. It is now housed within the Department of Housing and Urban Development, or HUD.

FHA also guarantees to the lender a certain portion of the mortgage amount should the loan default. The agency has a fee—similar to the VA funding fee—called the *mortgage insurance premium*, or MIP. The MIP is calculated at 1.50 percent of the loan and may also be included in the loan amount.

Although there is a minimum down payment for FHA loans, the minimum investment is just 3.50 percent.

FHA loans are easier to qualify for than conventional loans due to the lower down payment and relaxed income and credit guidelines. Although FHA loans are not for those with damaged credit, they are definitely more lenient from a credit perspective.

Rates for FHA mortgage are competitive with VA and conventional programs as well. In addition to the initial MIP, there is a monthly MIP payment that is made along with the mortgage payment that is calculated at $1/2$ percent of the loan amount. A typical monthly payment on a $200,000 sale price, 3.00 percent down, and a mortgage loan at 6.50 percent would look like this:

Sales Price	$200,000
Down Payment	$6,000
Loan Amount	$ 194,000
MIP (1.50%)	$2,910
Final Loan	$196,910

Monthly Payment at 6.50% on a 30-year mortgage

Principal and Interest	$1,244
Taxes (est.)	$167
MIP ($1/2$% on $194,000)	$80
Total	$1,491

Unlike VA loans, FHA loans aren't restricted to a certain group of people (including first-time buyers), and they don't impose income limitations. The only requirements are that you can't have more than one FHA loan at a time, the property must be owner-occupied, and the loan can't be used to purchase investment real estate.

There is one unique characteristic to FHA loans. They pertain to nonoccupying coborrowers, usually called "cosigners."

FHA is the only loan program that allows for cosigners to help the buyer qualify for the loan. Technically, other loan programs allow for cosigners, but in those cases the lender requires the owner-occupying buyer to qualify on his or her own, without the cosigners income. So there's no particular advantage to having a nonoccupying coborrower on a conventional loan.

Not so with FHA loans. In fact, the occupying buyer doesn't even need to have a job at all if the cosigners can qualify for the new mortgage on top of their current debt.

This is where the expression "kiddie-condo" comes from. Parents can cosign on the loan for their kids, make a low down payment, have the kids live there, and still get the best interest rates.

For a parent or a relative to help with a conventional loan, the rate could be $1/4$ to $3/8$ percent higher, along with a bigger down payment.

FHA loans have another unique feature when it comes to down payment funds: Conventional loans require that the buyers must have a minimum of 5 percent of their own funds in the transaction. FHA loans make allowances for down payment and even closing costs to be given to the buyer in the form of an outright gift with restrictions.

Gift funds for FHA loans can only be given by family members, employers, nonprofit organizations, religious institutions, trade unions, and domestic partners.

Although there are no income or first-time homebuyer limitations for an FHA loan, there are loan limits that will vary from county to county. FHA loan amounts are limited to 115 percent of the median home price of the area not to exceed $625,000. These strict loan limits can be exceeded only when rolling in the initial MIP. You can find out the loan limits in your area by visiting HUD's website at www.hud.gov.

Neither FHA nor VA loans are approved for co-op share financing, except for VA loans in New York City.

DOWN PAYMENT ASSISTANCE

There are other forms of government assistance that do not include actually making a mortgage loan but help with down payments and closing costs. Down payment assistance (DPA) can come in the form of a restricted grant or a loan to the buyer. The most common restriction is that the buyer can make no more than 100 percent of the median income for the area. If the median income is $50,000 for the area, to qualify for this assistance you can make no more than $50,000. Other programs may even require the buyer make less than 100 percent, with some programs restricting the benefit to those who make 80 percent of the median income for their area.

DPAs will require that you be a first-time homebuyer. How do DPAs make that determination? The DPA will follow the lead from your lender who will look first at your credit report to see if there is an outstanding mortgage or that you had one in the past. Lenders can also review your tax returns for the previous three years to see if you have taken any mortgage interest deductions.

For purposes of qualifying a first-time buyer, lenders only go back three years to see if any interest deductions have been taken.

DPAs will approve your down payment assistance application and send the qualifying amount to the closing table when you go to close on your condo. The lender approves the loan and the DPA agency makes sure the approved loan meets its own criteria.

Some DPAs from government agencies will issue funds up to a certain amount, say $10,000 for first-time buyers. This can be a loan or an outright grant with no repayment until or unless the property is sold.

It's important to note that even though a DPA may be available, the mortgage program you select may not accept it. Many conventional loans still require the buyer to have a minimum of 5 percent in the transaction.

Again, FHA loans shine in this regard because they don't require buyers to use their own funds as long as the funds in the transaction come from a qualifying source.

DPAs are typically issued through state or local government agencies. You can find DPAs by doing a quick Web search. Many larger cities have multiple DPA programs, so do your homework to find the right one for you and your new purchase.

| CHAPTER 5 |

Rules Governing Loans for Condos, Co-ops, and Townhouses

ALTHOUGH FANNIE MAE AND FHA have specific guidelines that lenders use to approve a buyer, these agencies also have certain distinctions between the various stages a condominium or townhouse might be in.

Condos can come in all shapes and sizes and can be as few as two units or a city skyscraper 50 stories high with hundreds of units. They can be built new or they can be converted from a previous structure such as an old apartment or office building.

Because condos can vary so much, Fannie Mae and FHA have rules that govern which types of condos loans can be made on and which ones cannot. Some condos can't qualify for conventional or government financing because the project doesn't have certain characteristics, such as a predominance of owner-occupants compared to units that are rented out.

Or there may be too much commercial activity or perhaps it's a condotel. But just as Fannie, Freddie, VA, and FHA have guidelines for buyers, they have strict guidelines for the project itself.

Fannie and Freddie, which set conventional guidelines, classify condos using "types" for Freddie and "classes" for Fannie. Each designation lets lenders know how to set about approving the condominium project so that the loans they issue are legitimate under conventional guidelines.

Fannie Mae and Freddie Mac used to approve condominium projects themselves using information provided to them by an individual lender or by a developer wishing to get Fannie Mae and Freddie Mac approval. When a condo project has approval from conventional or government guidelines, then the units retain their value because financing will be widely available through most mortgage lenders.

There are also two types of reviews: A limited review is when the lender answers a set of basic questions regarding the condo project; a full review is when the project undergoes a thorough examination of the building's history, engineering reports on the structure, evidence of legal transfer of ownership from the developer to the HOA, and so on. If a project does not have a prior approval from Fannie, Freddie, VA, or FHA, it may take too long to get approval in time to meet the contract date.

What is required in a full review? It's a lot, and it's why developers are supposed to get their project approved at the early stages of development. Sometimes they don't. And when that happens, unless the project is designated as a limited review project, it's not likely you'll get conventional or government financing.

Here is what is required in a full review:

➤ *Appraisal.* The developer must show the current value of the unit and also show that the unit meets certain guidelines, such as all units having separate meters for electricity and other utilities.

➤ *Minimum Insurance Coverage.* Condominium projects must have a minimum amount of insurance—not only to protect the structure itself, but also to protect the association from lawsuits. Most *liability* coverage requires at minimum $1 million in protection plus structural and common area protection. An insurance policy must include 100 percent replacement riders as well.

➤ *Legal.* Legal documents that conform to current guidelines must be reviewed by an attorney to certify that the project meets conventional and government guidelines.

➤ *HOA.* Lender will warrant that the HOA budget is adequate to cover reserves for replacement and maintenance of common areas such as sidewalks or swimming pools and have at least a 10 percent reserve set aside for deferred maintenance. Deferred maintenance items are those that need to be repaired to keep the value of the condo intact such as roofing, paint, windows, and such.

➤ *Occupancy.* At least 51 percent of the units must be owner-occupied or listed as vacation units (versus rental units).

➤ *Single Entity.* The lender must determine that no individual can own more than 10 percent of the units in the project. This is done by surveying ownership of the individual units or through verification from the HOA.

➤ **Delinquency.** No more than 15 percent of the units can be more than 30 days past due on their HOA dues.

➤ **Utility.** No more than 20 percent of the square footage of the project can be for nonresidential purposes.

Is that a mouthful, or what? Now let's add additional requirements for co-ops.

➤ **Marketability.** The project must be located in an area where there are other co-ops.

➤ **Completion.** The project cannot be subject to additional phases.

➤ **Occupancy.** Owner-occupancy requirements increase from 51 percent to 80 percent.

➤ **Ownership.** No individual may own more than 10 percent of the stock or shares of the cooperative.

➤ **Facilities.** Amenities such as parking or workout facilities must be owned by the co-op.

➤ **Commercial.** Any commercial spaces must be compatible with the surrounding project and market, and any income to the co-op cannot exceed 20 percent of its total income.

➤ **Financials.** It must be shown that the co-ops budget is such that it is able to meet current and future operating expenses.

➤ **Management.** It must be shown that there is an adequate management team in place. Professional management companies manage most co-ops. If this is the case, the contract with the management company can't have a prepayment penalty if the contract is cancelled.

Is this enough? Full reviews are onerous, and if the project you're thinking of buying doesn't already have a conventional or government approval, then you're going to have your work cut out for you. This list takes some time, effort, and resources to get a project approved.

A limited review is much less invasive and can be performed in a relatively short time, as the lender goes down a simplified list of questions. This questionnaire is sent to the HOA for it to complete. A typical questionnaire asks for the following information:

1. What is the total number of units in project?
2. What is the total number of units sold or under contract?
3. What is the total number of units rented?
4. How many phases are there?
5. Is subject phase complete?
6. Are all the common areas complete?
7. Does any single entity own more than 10 percent of the units?
8. Is there a lobby with a rental desk?
9. Are short-term rentals allowed?
10. Are there time-share arrangements?
11. Is the HOA involved in any litigation?
12. What percentage of owners are more than 30 days *delinquent* on HOA dues?

The HOA would answer these questions and return the form to the lender, who would review the answers to make sure they comply with condo guidelines. The lender would then examine the insurance policy to make sure that the property is properly covered. With a limited review, the condo or townhouse project isn't universally approved, meaning anyone who wishes to finance a unit in the project won't have to go through the project-approval process. The lender will place a loan for that individual purchase. Limited reviews typically require a minimum of 20 percent down.

This method of approval is sometimes called a "spot" approval. It is used when Fannie, Freddie, VA, or FHA hasn't yet approved the property.

Finally, there is an expedited approval process using Fannie's online project approval method (Condo Project Manager, or CPM). This is an online process of approving condos that provides lender-specific project acceptance.

Property classes and types are important because it may mean you have to put more down. It may also mean that you can't get conventional approval at all. Co-ops, in particular, have only one review process—the full review—if you want to get conventional financing. If the co-op doesn't meet Fannie guidelines, then conventional financing won't work and you must go with a portfolio lender.

Because Freddie Mac, FHA, and the VA do not offer financing for co-ops, Fannie is the only conventional source of funds for these properties.

Fannie Mae offers the following condo types:

Type P   Limited Review for New Project

Type Q   Established Project or Established Two- to Four-Unit Project

Type R   CPM Expedited Review or Lender Full-Review New Project

Type S   CPM Expedited Review or Lender Full-Review Established Project

Type U   FHA-Approved Project

Freddie Mac, the other conventional loan type, used to categorize condos by classes but now simplifies condo types into the following two types: established and new construction.

Established condominiums require that ownership of the condos be transferred to the HOA from the developer and meet the same general guidelines as Fannie types. New construction also follows similar guidelines as Fannie Mae.

In fact, Fannie, Freddie, and FHA can have reciprocal approvals where one agency will automatically approve a project that was previously approved by the other two.

There's an exception: projects using VA financing (because the VA still approves condo projects independent of any lender). And remember, neither FHA, VA, nor Freddie Mac makes allowances for co-ops.

For years, classifying condominiums was a real burden. Sometimes developers wouldn't go through the tedious process of getting their project approved and would leave it up to the buyers to get their own financing. Or they might arrange financing with a local bank or lender. But gradually the condo approval process eased, making buying and financing a condo much easier.

If the project does receive approval, it is deemed "warrantable," meaning that the lender warrants that the project meets condo guidelines. If the project does not meet condo guidelines, the condo is then labeled as "unwarrantable."

WARRANTABLE VERSUS NONWARRANTABLE PROJECTS

When your property is *warrantable*, you can have a bevy of loan choices from a variety of lenders. You're free to shop around for the best loan from the best mortgage company.

A *nonwarrantable* status means you don't have that luxury. Instead, you are limited to certain lenders and banks that offer nonwarrantable loans.

Nonwarrantable status will typically require a minimum of 25 percent down and will be approximately $1/2$ percent higher in interest rate. Because co-ops must have a full review if they do not meet Fannie standards, conventional lending will not be an option.

That being said, co-ops understand conventional guidelines—or at least they should. Many will work to achieve and maintain a warrantable status to make the units more marketable. When a unit is more marketable, its value increases.

Nonwarrantable can mean just one item on a checklist doesn't make the grade. For instance, there are 100 units in a project and one person owns 12 units, or 12 percent of the project. That would make the project nonwarrantable, requiring a higher down payment and a higher rate to go along with it.

Another example of a nonwarrantable condo often occurs in two- to four-unit projects. Duplexes or fourplexes can be turned into condos, but doing so may skew the percent-of-ownership requirement. In the case of a two-unit condo, each owner would own 50 percent of the project and 25 percent of a four-unit project.

Sometimes a nonwarrantable can turn into a warrantable because of the dynamics of the project itself, for instance, if the association was in some type of litigation but that was no longer the case or units that were previously rented out were purchased and occupied by the buyers.

The importance of project approval cannot be stressed enough, because once the project has received approval, it's approved from that point on.

Fannie Mae, Freddie Mac, VA, and FHA all have online databases of approved condo projects. You should consult these databases when shopping so you'll know in advance the types of financing that may be available to you.

FHA also has a spot-approval process for a previously unapproved project. But the requirements for the spot approval make it nearly impossible to obtain spot approval! FHA spot-approval requirements are:

1. Total number of units in project
2. Total number of units sold and closed
3. Total number of units under contract pending
4. Total number of units owner-occupied
5. Any entity owns more than 10 percent of the units
6. Is there a right of first refusal clause in the HOA documents?

7. All owners share common areas equally
8. Is the subject phase complete, including common areas?
9. Any current special assessments, and if so, how much?
10. Any current or pending litigation?
11. Has the HOA controlled the association for one year?
12. Any adverse environmental factors?
13. All units owned fee simple (not leasehold)
14. Does HOA have a reserve plan and a reserve fund separate from the operating account and is the fund adequate to cover deferred maintenance?
15. How much is in the reserve fund?
16. How many units currently have FHA financing?

I realize it's a long list, but it's usually only items 14, 15, and 16 that pull the plug on most FHA spot approvals. That the list is "lender delegated" means the lender that is requesting a spot approval must certify to HUD that the condo project meets FHA requirements.

Condo associations typically don't have a reserve plan and a reserve fund separate from operating expenses. An HOA fund has one big pile of money that is monitored and expensed either by the HOA or the HOA's management or accounting firm.

If they do in fact have a separate reserve, the lender must certify that it is sufficient to cover any deferred maintenance. But how would an association know that? And how would a lender know how to determine whether the fund was sufficient? If a lender warrants that a project meets FHA guidelines when in fact it doesn't, the lender loses the FHA loan guarantee should the loan ever go bad.

Even if the lender were to make that determination, it's the last one, determining how many units currently have FHA financing, that's the real deal breaker. HOAs may know how many units are sold, but they typically do not know the type of financing a buyer has. True, mortgage loans are a matter of public record, so the lender or the association or even a title company could do some legwork. But that would mean researching every single unit to determine how many are financed with FHA loans.

The FHA says these are not hard and fast rules and that lenders must show "due diligence" in trying to answer these final three questions. Although that seems fair to the lender, you'll be hard pressed to find a lender willing to claim due diligence, because that can be a moving target.

Lenders will err on the side of caution and not perform an FHA spot approval. Okay, they *might*, but I've never heard of one.

FHA loans are attractive for a variety of reasons, mainly the minimal down payment required. And even that down payment can be in the form of a *gift* or grant.

If you're interested in an FHA loan due to the low amount of funds required to close, visit www.hud.gov and search for FHA-approved properties in the area where you want to live.

When you visit HUD's website, you can search by city, by state, or by ZIP code. When you enter the city or town where you want to live, you'll get a list of all FHA-approved properties. This is where you begin your search. If you can't find any FHA-approved units to your liking, be prepared to put more money down and go conventional. The ideal choice here is to try FHA first, then Fannie Mae.

Fannie Mae's spot-approval process is much easier than FHA's. Even if a project isn't Fannie Mae–approved when you first search, as long as the project is completed, all common areas are done, the majority of the units are owner-occupied, and so on, you should be fine.

Although condos and townhouses can have various classes assigned to them and be deemed warrantable or nonwarrantable, cooperatives don't carry that many distinctions. Either they're Fannie approved and a class is assigned to them or they're not approved and you'll need to go to a bank that has co-op loans in its portfolio. That doesn't mean the co-op won't have to pass similar occupancy requirements or have a responsible governing board. It will also have to carry adequate insurance, just as a warrantable condo or townhouse would.

Banks will want to make sure they're making a solid loan on a marketable "share" and will review the project just like any other. Because co-ops and co-op lenders are typically concentrated in geographical areas—downtown Manhattan, for instance—it's likely that almost any bank in the area that makes mortgage loans participates in the co-op financing market. So it's likely that various banks and lenders in town already approve the co-op you're considering buying into. That means the cooperative is already warrantable from a lender's perspective.

CHAPTER 6

The Impact of Credit on Your Ability to Buy a Condo, Co-op, or Townhouse

MUCH HAS CHANGED OVER THE YEARS with regard to credit and how it affects a buyer's ability to purchase real estate. One's debt ratio may be in line or one may have a good-sized down payment, but if there is a problem with a buyer's credit, then having good income with a good down payment won't matter.

Credit can impact the interest rate you get on a mortgage. And perhaps more important, it can determine whether you can get a mortgage at all.

First though, exactly what is credit? Simply, it's the ability and the willingness of a person to repay a debt.

Ability is having the necessary income or assets available to pay back a loan. You have to have a job of some sorts or have income from other sources such as interest and dividend income or spousal support, for instance.

Ability is sometimes expressed as a percent, as we discussed when explaining debt ratios. Typical debt ratios, front and back, historically have been somewhere around 33/41, meaning 33 percent of your gross income can go toward housing and 41 percent of your gross income can go toward housing and all other installment and revolving debt.

If your debt ratios were, say, 90, then a lender would determine that in fact you don't have the ability to repay the debt because you don't have enough money. What is the highest debt ratio a lender will allow?

Some loan programs have specific ratio guidelines, say, 45; but many don't have a specific percentage for a debt ratio. Rather, they factor in the debt ratio as part of the overall approval process.

Higher income borrowers can have higher allowable debt ratios than lower income borrowers. I've approved mortgage loans with debt ratios in the 60s, for example. It's not necessarily that rich people are getting a favor and others are getting the shaft. Instead it's due to *disposable income.*

Disposable income is the amount of money left over every month to goof around with—go to the movies, fill up the car with gas, or invest in a retirement fund. Higher income folks will have more disposable income to pay the phone bill or have the dog groomed.

Say that a debt ratio is at 60. Let's apply that ratio to someone who makes $40,000 per year and someone who makes $250,000 per year.

The amount $40,000 per year works to $3,333 per month. A 60 debt ratio means that 60 percent of $3,333 is already allocated to bills, or about $2,000. That leaves us with $1,333 for other things. If you subtract approximate withholdings for federal and state income taxes and Social Security, you might have $2,500 left for bills. If $2,000 were reserved for debt, that would leave only about $500 for the borrower to pay for food, gasoline, and utilities (not to mention the occasional pizza or movie).

Lenders won't allow borrowers who are not rich to have such a high debt ratio.

Now examine a debt ratio of 60 on a $250,000 income. Monthly, that's $20,833 and 60 percent of that is $12,499 per month. Even after taxes, there's still more discretionary income available for things such as pizza, parties, and movies.

The other side of the credit coin is the absolute willingness to repay a debt. The borrower has the money, but does he pay his bills on time, every time?

I recall a client that was a vice president of a publicly traded corporation. He made a lot of money. But he had damaged his credit by letting bills slip by and not paying them on time. He was never really in debt; he could certainly pay his bills, but for whatever reason he would let some slide every now and then. And it hurt his credit. He probably should have hired an accountant to take care of all his personal stuff.

He certainly had the ability, but not necessarily the willingness, to pay his bills on time.

How do you establish credit? You may hear something such

as, "You have to have credit to get credit," and that's partially true. If you've never applied for credit anywhere, then perhaps the easiest account to establish would be one from a department store such as Sears or JCPenney.

You're likely to get approved with a small credit line of, say, $500. Then the department store will sit back and see how you handle your new responsibility. Charge something and then pay it back when you get your first statement. That's pretty much about it.

After about 12 months, the department store will review your payment history and see that you have used the card and paid back the balance responsibly. Then it'll offer you a higher credit limit. That's how you can start a credit history.

Credit unions are also a good way to start a credit profile. They have programs to help their members obtain and establish a credit history.

For those who do not have current credit accounts and are just starting out, FHA allows for "nontraditional" credit. This form of credit is not reported on any credit report. Rather, it's a review of other items that will show a pattern of paying bills on time.

If you have no credit accounts whatsoever, a lender can evaluate timely payment with things such as your telephone bill, utility bill, or cable bill. Most important, the lender will want to see 12 months of consecutive timely rent payments by reviewing copies, front and back, of your rent checks or money orders.

Credit histories are stored in three major databases (also called repositories) run by companies called Experian, Equifax, and Transunion. These companies store and report the credit histories of consumers in the United States.

Prior to these repositories, when a business was considering extending credit to a customer, the business would go through a painstaking process of contacting other businesses that had extended credit to their potential customer and get a report on their credit history.

The business would ask the following questions:

> ➤ Did you extend credit to this person?
> ➤ Did she pay you back on time?
> ➤ How much credit did you give her?
> ➤ What is the current balance owed to you?
> ➤ What is the minimum monthly payment that she makes?
> ➤ How long has she been a credit customer?
> ➤ Is the account currently in good standing?
> ➤ Has she ever been above her credit limit?

These are just a few of the questions a business might ask. The business would then repeat the process, typically by mailing a form to be completed, to other businesses where the potential customer had opened credit.

But with a repository, the business only has to make one stop to collect the data reported by other businesses. Everything you've ever done when opening a credit account is reported to these credit repositories by the business that issued you credit.

CHECK YOUR CREDIT FIRST

Before you get too far in the process, you need to see what your potential lender will see, so you need to get a copy of your credit report before you apply for any mortgage loan.

I know this is probably not the first time you've heard this advice, but it still surprises me when people don't review their credit before applying for a mortgage.

There seems to be no end to companies that want to provide you with a free credit report as long as you subscribe to whatever credit service they're offering. The most common pitch is from companies that want to monitor your credit for you by letting you know when other companies are looking at your credit without your direct permission.

How can companies look at your credit data without your permission? These repositories have legal agreements with other credit issuers to which they sell data. When you get a credit card offer in the mail, or a solicitation for an automobile loan, it's because that credit issuer has paid for the privilege of seeing whether you have good credit. This is perfectly legal. And although it may be annoying sometimes, it does facilitate the issuance of credit. Whether people use that credit wisely is another issue.

A new trend regarding credit solicitations is via what is called "trigger" leads. A trigger lead is a lead sold to mortgage companies. It was so named because the lead is triggered when a consumer makes a mortgage application with a lender. When a mortgage lender or mortgage broker requests a credit report to evaluate, that request can turn into the form of a lead that can be sold to other mortgage companies.

Obviously, if a mortgage company is requesting a credit report on a particular borrower, then that person is seeking a mortgage. The repository sells these leads to other mortgage companies in lightning-quick fashion.

Some mortgage companies that buy trigger leads are made up of telephone sales reps that call you within hours after the initial credit request was made.

"Hi David, this is ABC Mortgage Company, and we're calling to see if we can be of any assistance today should you be thinking of refinancing or buying real estate."

You might think that was an incredible coincidence, But in reality, it's nothing more than someone buying leads from a repository.

It goes without saying that in no way should you ever use someone who simply calls you out of the blue wanting to finance your property. You've already done your homework as outlined in chapter 3.

Where do you get your credit report to review? You can certainly subscribe to those various companies that want to monitor your credit for you, but that costs money. Alternatively, you can get one free credit report from each repository once every 12 months.

The three bureaus have established, at the federal government's request, a website where consumers can go to get their credit report. This site is at www.annualcreditreport.com. There are similar sounding websites that try and mimic the name to trick consumers into thinking they are going to a website that offers free credit reports and credit-monitoring services.

When you get your credit report, your next step is to review it. What to look for? Mistakes. Mistakes that show someone else's credit information on your credit report are good ones to check for. Is there a credit account showing up and you have no idea whom it belongs to?

Unfortunately, when three different credit bureaus try and track everything you've ever done credit-wise in your entire consumer life, it's possible mistakes will be made. Once you have an accepted sales contract and you have to close within 30 days, there might not be enough time to fix the errors to satisfy the lender.

Do you have a name that may be more common than others? Is your first name Bob? Last name Jones? Then there's a greater chance of errors on your credit report simply because there are so many Bob Joneses in your town.

Another common mistake found on credit reports is accounts that appear to be open when in fact they have been paid and perhaps closed. If you had a collection account that you paid off, it's still possible one or more of the bureaus are still reporting that account as outstanding.

These bureaus do nothing except collect the data. They don't go out and verify it. Even if you paid off a collection account, if the business that reported the outstanding balance never contacted the bureaus to tell them that you settled the account, the bureaus would never know. In that case, it would be reported as still being outstanding.

Even if only one of the three bureaus has the closed account listed as outstanding, you'll still be required to provide proof that the information being reported is incorrect.

Finally, another area where incorrect information can be reported is in the "Public Records" section, located near the very end of your report. Here is where any tax liens or judgments would be reported. Old tax liens can show up on your report, and you'd never know it. A tax *lien* can be filed for overdue federal and state taxes; it can also show up when it involves delinquent property taxes.

A credit report can include your name, Social Security number, address, and even your previous employers.

The report will show the active accounts first, ones that are currently opened or being used. The report shows the following information:

- ➤ Business name that issued the credit
- ➤ Date the account was opened
- ➤ Account number
- ➤ Date information reported
- ➤ Last activity
- ➤ Credit limit
- ➤ Highest balance
- ➤ Number of months reviewed
- ➤ Current balance
- ➤ How many times past due
- ➤ Minimum monthly payment

That's a lot of information. Combine that with three different bureaus and people with similar names and you can see why mistakes can sometimes happen. It's not right that they happen, but they do. It's a business's responsibility to accurately report a customer's credit activity. Yet, sometimes it fails to do just that.

How can a bureau have information in it, correct or not, that is different from what the other bureaus are reporting? These three repositories are located in different parts of the country. Experian has a reporting branch in Texas. Transunion is based in Pennsylvania. And Equifax reports out of Georgia.

Local businesses may report to one bureau but may not report to the other two. National business will typically report to all three bureaus, but many smaller businesses only need to subscribe to one credit bureau (it's less expensive), so naturally that business would choose the bureau closest to it that would reflect local credit issuers as well as national ones.

FIND OUT YOUR CREDIT SCORES

Much has been made about credit scores and how important they are to you. A credit score is a number that is calculated to predict the likelihood of default on a loan. The higher the credit score, the better the credit.

Credit scores can range from as low as 300 to as high as 850. I've never witnessed a "perfect" credit score, which leads me to believe it's a theoretical number that can never be reached. The highest score that I recall seeing during my years as a loan officer was around 820.

Credit scoring has been around for years, but it became important to the mortgage lending industry in the late 1990s. Each *credit repository* issues its own credit score, so you should have three scores in all.

Each repository, Equifax, Experian, and Transunion, calculates a credit score on its own using a system devised by *Fair Isaac Corporation,* commonly called *FICO.* FICO is a registered trademark.

This special algorithm is licensed to the three bureaus by FICO, which in turn will provide those numbers to the mortgage lender or mortgage broker when asked. It's important to note that these three bureaus have developed their own internal credit-scoring model.

Other third-party businesses also advertise free credit reports with credit scores, but you can't be sure if the score you're getting is the same one those bureaus use when reporting to a mortgage lender.

You might for instance get a credit score of 700 from a website. But this number is different from the ones generated by FICO programs. So, you could be misled into thinking your credit score is 700 when it is actually 600.

On the other hand, you could find out that your credit score obtained directly from the bureau is 600 when in fact your credit score is much higher than that. If you get false information about your score that results in your believing your score is too low, then you might not apply for a mortgage at all.

Credit scores are made up of many different factors, all of which apply to your ability and willingness to repay a debt. But some factors weigh more heavily than others. The key ingredients to a credit score are:

- ➤ Payment history
- ➤ Available credit
- ➤ Length of time you've had credit
- ➤ Credit inquiries
- ➤ Types of credit

Payment History

This is the "willingness" section and shows if you've ever been late on an account, how much your payments are/were, what your past and present balances were/are, and whether you've ever exceeded your credit limit. Payment history is the single biggest factor when determining a credit score. It makes up 35 percent of your score.

That means up to 297 "points" can be awarded to your credit score since 35 percent of the maximum 850 is 297.

But what, exactly, is "late" when it comes to credit reporting? Being late means a payment that is more than 30+, 60+, 90+, and 120+ days late. It does not mean that if your car payment is due on the 15th and you paid it on the 16th then you had a late payment. Late payments will not hurt your credit score even up to 29 days past due.

Be forewarned; most revolving credit accounts will hit you with higher rates and penalties if you don't pay the minimum amount on or before your due date. But for the purposes of calculating a credit score for a mortgage application, the pain starts on day 31.

It also follows that your score will get hurt even more if you were more than 60 days past due compared to 30; 90 days past due compared to 60; and 120 days or more past due compared to 90. If your account got more than 120 days past due, then it's likely the account turned into a collection account, where the credit issuer has closed the account and is now trying to collect the balance owed.

A collection account will hurt your credit score more than a 120-day late payment. If collection efforts fail, then the credit grantor will likely "charge off" the account, which means it's given up on collecting directly. Then finally a business can take you to court and sue you to obtain a "judgment."

A charge-off will hurt your score more than a collection. And a judgment will hurt your score more than a charge-off.

Available Credit

Available credit is the second most important scoring category, representing 30 percent, or 255 possible points for your score. Available credit is defined as the percentage of current balances compared to current credit limits assigned to those accounts.

For example, if you have a credit card with a credit limit of $1,000 and a balance of $700, then the available credit will be 30 percent. If you have a credit limit of $1,000 and a balance of $300, then your available credit will be 70 percent.

The magical number is 70 percent to optimize this part of your credit score. This also puts to rest the myth that it's best for consumers to close out credit accounts they no longer need nor use. Although that may have been a prudent gesture 20 years ago, closing unused accounts can actually harm a credit score instead of helping.

Here's the thinking: To determine prudent credit patterns, you need to borrow money. How would a lender determine your ability and willingness to pay them back if you've never borrowed before? That's why credit scoring puts a high emphasis on carrying a small balance relative to one's available credit. If you have old credit accounts with no balances, it may not look good. If you want to optimize your credit score, you should keep your balances to around 30 percent of your available credit.

Let's look at an example. Say you have three credit cards, each with a $10,000 limit, giving you a $30,000 credit line. If you have a zero balance on all three cards, your credit score won't improve. But if you buy a car with one of those cards and now have a $10,000 balance, your score will begin to improve because your balance is now 30 percent of your available credit.

On the other hand, once you begin to reach your credit limit, your score will begin to deteriorate. When your balances approach 50 percent of your available credit on a regular basis, your scores will begin to drop. Worse, if your balances actually exceed your credit limits your scores will drop even further.

Now let's say you have those three credit accounts—each with a $10,000 limit and a $10,000 balance. If you cancelled one of those cards, you would have a $20,000 limit with a $10,000 balance, or 50 percent available. Your scores would not improve and might begin to fall. If you cancelled the second account, you would have a $10,000 limit and a $10,000 balance and your scores will fall.

It's also important to note that if you have an open account you must occasionally use the account or the credit history won't be counted; it will become "dormant" in the eyes of the scoring model. If your goal is to obtain the highest score possible, you'll need to use one of these credit accounts every so often to include the account's history in your credit score.

You can also hurt your score when any single account hits its limit, regardless of other available credit. This can come into play when you receive a credit card offer in the mail that wants you to transfer all your old balances to its zero-interest credit card.

Makes sense, doesn't it? Open up a new account and transfer all your old balances into a new one with no interest? Who cares if it's only for a year? Think of the money you'll save!

Guess what? If you transfer all your balances, you'd better make sure your new zero-interest account leaves you with at least 50 percent of available credit. Otherwise your score will be damaged if you transfer $30,000 into a new credit card with a $30,000 limit.

Length of Time You've Had Credit

The longer you've been a consumer with credit accounts, the higher your score will be. Points are awarded a credit score for extended credit histories, as long as the credit history is good. Extended patterns of bad credit behavior, regardless of how long the accounts have been opened, won't help a score. But long histories of timely payment will elevate a credit score.

Fifteen percent of a credit score, or a possible 127 points, can be awarded for length of credit histories.

Credit Inquiries

How often you apply for credit accounts for 10 percent of your total score. The more times you apply for credit, the more it hurts your score.

When someone is applying for numerous credit accounts, it can be a signal that the consumer is in over her head. She might be applying for credit to pay bills. Or perhaps she bought an automobile that squeezed her budget each month until she began paying everyday bills with credit cards.

Remember, companies can look at your credit without your knowing about it to see if they want to issue you a credit card. These are called "soft" inquiries and do not count in the credit-scoring model.

Nor do consumer inquiries where consumers check their own credit for errors by logging on to www.annualcredit report.com, for instance.

A "hard" inquiry is when the consumer makes a direct request for credit. What happens when someone applies for a mortgage with two or three different companies at the same time? Applying for credit for the same purchase at the same time would be considered a single inquiry. Applying for credit over an extended period, say 60 or 90 days, would be viewed as multiple inquiries and can hurt a score.

When you apply for employment somewhere, the employer may run a credit report on you. This, too, would be considered a soft inquiry. Same with other organizations such as insurance companies that run credit reports for purposes other than issuing credit.

Types of Credit

This final category, which makes up the final 10 percent of the score, reviews the various credit accounts as to the type of credit issued and who issued it. A class of credit companies known as "Finance Agencies" offers credit to those with subpar credit histories or for those who have a hard time obtaining credit. Having a credit account from a finance agency won't necessarily damage a score, but the payment histories on them won't help a credit score as much as a traditional credit account.

The best credit account to have? A mortgage. Timely payments on a mortgage is the single best account to have on a credit report.

CREDIT SCORE FACTS AND FALLACIES

Although these factors make up a credit score, the exact algorithm developed by FICO is an unknown to the consumer. In fact, the scoring method is tweaked at times if there appear to be inconsistencies or consumers have found ways to cheat the system.

For instance, it became known that being an authorized user on a credit card account would help a person's score, if the account was in good standing.

Say that a parent had excellent credit with scores in the 800s. By putting his son on the credit card account as an authorized user, whether the son ever received a credit card from his parent's account to use, the son would soon see his scores begin to go up because his parent's credit patterns from that credit card would transfer to him.

The son would see the benefit of his parent's credit histories without establishing any credit himself. There were even advertisements to folks with damaged credit, encouraging them to become authorized users on cards belonging to people they would never even meet—as long as they paid a fee. The authorized user would never get a credit card but would, in fact, get the benefit of that credit card's payment history. This was an oversight in FICO's scoring model that was soon corrected.

FICO keeps its scoring model locked deep in its closet, but individuals are always trying to figure out any idiosyncrasies to game the system. There are some general things we know about the FICO model, such as which factors weigh more heavily on computing a credit score, but the permutations of all the possible combinations would be nearly impossible to calculate. But there are some things we do know.

Credit scores pay close attention to the most recent 24-month history and less so beyond that. Even with a bankruptcy or collection accounts in the past. For instance, a few years ago a guy got hurt in an automobile accident and was unable to work for several months and got behind on his bills. Some of them even went to collection, and he saw his credit scores tumble. His scores went from 740 to 580 in a heartbeat.

But he got back on his feet and returned to work. He began to pay off his collection accounts and got caught up on his other accounts and paid his balances down. His scores didn't improve immediately, but eventually they did after about 18 months.

Scoring models don't work with an isolated incident. Rather, they try and determine if there's a pattern beginning to emerge in a credit file. One late payment by itself won't damage a credit score much, but several late payments over an extended period certainly will because it shows a pattern.

Credit scores are designed to reflect the likelihood of default. And recent history is more of an indicator than something that happened 10 years ago.

Even though you get three credit scores, one from each bureau, the lender will throw out the highest and the lowest—and will use the middle score. They're not averaged together as some think. Nor are two people's credit scores averaged when they apply for a mortgage together.

If a couple were to apply together for a mortgage, that would make for six credit scores, right? Lenders would look at the lowest of the middle scores for each applicant. If the husband has a 720 middle score and the wife has a 520 score, they might not get approved because the lender would use the 520 score for purposes of underwriting the loan.

In this instance it might be possible to have the husband apply for the loan on his own and leave his wife off the loan entirely. Her credit score and her credit rating would be off the table.

As long as the husband's income is sufficient to buy the property and still have acceptable debt ratios, then the husband can be on the mortgage by himself. However, if the wife's income is needed to obtain acceptable debt ratios and she has poor credit, the loan would be declined due to low scores.

Often, a dispute with a creditor shows on the credit report. A common dispute I've seen is from tenants breaking their lease with a landlord. The former renter may think that he or she will simply lose the deposit and move on. But some apartment management companies will still want the money for the months remaining on the lease.

The consumer applies for credit and sees a collection account with his former landlord. Perhaps the consumer disagrees because he gave his 30-day notice and he lost his deposit. But the apartment is still trying to collect two months of rent. The consumer doesn't budge, but on the advice of a friend, writes a letter to the credit bureaus explaining his side of the story.

This is called a "dispute" letter and is kept in the consumer's file for all potential lenders to review. In fact, now the credit report will read something like "Consumer Dispute" to let a lender know the consumer disagrees with the report.

But this is old school. Lenders don't read letters anymore. In fact, they usually just rely on the score and don't even review credit reports. Credit scores are pulled electronically; there's no protocol for reading a dispute letter. So, although it's perfectly legal to write one, it is likely a waste of time.

CREDIT SCORES AND QUALIFYING

In recent years, credit scores have become more of a factor in mortgage lending. Before, conventional and government loans didn't have a minimum score to get approved. The person trying to obtain the loan had only to obtain a loan approval from an automated underwriting system, or AUS. As long as the AUS issued the approval, the loan was eligible.

AUSs began to take hold in the late 1990s. Underwriting is the process of examining income, credit, assets, and all the other loan-approval factors piecemeal by hand.

Automated underwriting means the loan application is entered electronically into the AUS, which immediately reviews the various loan factors in the application while simultaneously pulling all three credit reports and all three credit scores.

Almost every loan submitted today is approved electronically. After the approval is issued, the underwriter simply verifies the information that is entered on the application. If the borrower says she makes $5,000 per month, the underwriter will want to see a pay stub reflecting that information. If the application says there is $30,000 in the bank, the underwriter will want to see bank statements showing $30,000 in an account.

Fannie Mae, Freddie Mac, FHA, and VA all use automated underwriting. Even portfolio lenders will use one of these systems to obtain an initial decision.

As with credit scores, automated underwriting has several variables that affect the approvability of a loan application. An AUS won't decline a loan because of a low credit score, but it may decline a loan due to damaged credit.

Sometimes, however, an AUS can be "tweaked" to obtain an approval. For instance, let's say a loan was run through the AUS with 5 percent down and is declined. The loan officer can adjust the loan application and run it through again with a "what-if" scenario. In this example, the loan officer could run the application with 10 percent down instead of 5.

If the loan is still declined, the loan officer could put 20 percent down in the application to see what happens. The application is run through the AUS with 20 percent down and gets an approval. Now we have a loan approval as long as we can come up with 20 percent down. What if we don't have that?

Then you can try and adjust other factors such as lowering an interest rate that would affect debt ratios or simply lowering the loan amount by buying a less expensive property.

But lenders have begun to tighten the reins on their loan approvals and put credit score restrictions on their approvals, regardless of what the AUS returned.

Now, along with AUS approval, a minimum credit score of 620 is required for all conventional loans. In addition to the minimum credit score required, additional penalties may be added when credit scores dip below 700.

A common penalty is $1/2$ of a discount point, or $1/8$ percent for each 20 points below 700.

On the other hand, loans with scores above 720 can find lenders who offer additional discounts to their rates, with a credit of $1/4$ point.

FHA lenders can have different minimum credit score requirements, but a common minimum score is 580 for an FHA loan approval. Other lenders will take an FHA loan with a credit score as low as 540 as long as it is accompanied by an AUS approval.

REPAIRING CREDIT

What do you do if your credit is in poor shape? First, try for an FHA approval. Although FHA is not designed for people with bad credit, it is much more lenient and minimum credit score requirements are less stringent. But if you're still in bad shape and you can't get an FHA loan, then you're going to need to take steps to reestablish credit and work to repair the damaged credit items.

If your scores are low, it's likely that your bad credit experiences were recent, within the past two years or so. Most people with bad credit started with good credit, and then something bad happened, such as a loss of job, a divorce, or a death in the family. Tragic events all, but not something that can't be overcome. But first let's examine true mistakes, reporting errors, and how to properly fix them.

Once you find out that your credit is less than stellar, suddenly be attuned to credit repair companies' advertisements: "Let us legally fix your credit!" or some such promise. Although the credit repair companies can in fact help repair credit, they can't do anything you can't do on your own.

One method these companies use is the "30 days or remove" tactic. By law, the three credit reporting agencies are required to validate the questionable item within 30 days or remove it from the credit report entirely.

For instance, you see that a collection account from an old cell phone company has appeared on your credit report and you think it's not yours. The credit repair agency will contact the bureau with a standard dispute letter that cites the federal law about removing information from credit files within 30 days if it can't be verified.

Once the request is received, the bureau will contact your old phone company or its collection agency. The bureau will ask if the negative information belongs to you. And if so, can they prove it? The collection company will typically respond with something to the effect of: "Yes, this information is valid. Here's a copy of the contract with his Social Security number."

Or not. If the account can't be confirmed, the credit repair agency will demand that the negative item be removed from the credit report. Then, the credit repair agency repeats the effort with the other two bureaus in similar fashion.

Sometimes the credit repair company will repeatedly ask the bureau to validate the same account—hoping the bureau will fail to do so within 30 days. If that happens, even if the account was valid, it may be legally removed!

Credit repair companies don't work for free. Typically, they collect money up front; after that, they may not follow through and actually do anything for you. Consequently, these companies don't enjoy a good reputation. If you do have a legitimate claim you should dispute the information yourself directly with the bureau.

You can go online at the various bureaus' websites or you can call them on the phone. But the best way to dispute an item is to write a letter identifying the offending account. Send the letter via overnight mail and get a signature upon delivery. Once they sign the form, the 30-day clock begins to tick—and you have a record.

On the 31st day, if the creditor hasn't asked for an extension (they can get an automatic 15-day extension), then you demand the item be removed. By law they must do it.

Credit bureaus haven't gotten many awards for customer service and they can be very bureaucratic. Just call their 1-800 number and see what I mean. You're likely to be solicited to join their credit-monitoring service. Then you'll talk to a customer service representative who cannot get the mistake fixed.

The fact is, if your credit report contains a mistake, the best way to get it fixed is by having your loan officer do it for you.

That's right: your loan officer. Remember, credit bureaus are for-profit enterprises. They make money by storing and reporting consumer credit histories. And they get lots and lots of business from mortgage companies. These agencies even hire sales representatives to solicit business from mortgage companies.

Credit-reporting agencies all offer the same service: providing credit reports and credit scores. To add value, they need to provide additional services to lenders.

So, instead of waiting 30 days to see if a bureau will remove a mistaken item, take your documentation to your loan officer. She will contact the credit bureau and forward the documentation to the right person there.

Once the credit agency reviews the item and confirms it doesn't belong there, it removes it. Just like that—in a matter of minutes. The negative item is removed and the credit company issues a new report.

But sometimes you need to take it one step further and address the credit score as well. It's possible that your credit score was calculated using the bad data. So, you'll need to make sure a new credit score is issued as well.

Credit bureaus have a feature called a *rapid rescore* that they offer to lenders that will not only remove the bad information but also recalculate the credit score as if the bad information were never there.

This is critical if your score is too low to qualify for financing. This service isn't free to your lender; rapid scores cost up to $50 per account per bureau. When a mistake appears on a credit report, the FICO scoring model can't determine whether it's an error; if it's on the report, it's calculated as part of the total credit score.

This is a common problem for people who have experienced bankruptcies. During a bankruptcy, credit accounts are either discharged or paid back over time. When the bankruptcy discharges old debts, sometimes the accounts aren't properly reported as having been included in a bankruptcy; instead they still show as outstanding accounts, even though the old debts are no longer legally valid. The big problem with such an occurrence is when a credit report shows a past bankruptcy and a current outstanding collections account. One of the worst things that can happen to a credit score is to have negative information in a credit file after a bankruptcy has been discharged.

Day after day, the credit score is getting hammered, all without the consumer's knowledge. The consumer thinks his credit is being repaired as the bankruptcy recedes further and further into the past. But in reality the credit is becoming worse and worse.

This is where a rapid rescore can help. Provide a copy of the bankruptcy discharge papers to your loan officer. She will forward the documentation showing that the offending accounts were included in the bankruptcy and aren't outstanding.

A rapid rescore will review the bankruptcy papers, remove the items, and run another series of credit scores as if the mistakes were never there. I have personally seen credit scores improve by more than 100 points in this fashion.

When the items are in fact not mistakes but are legitimate, the best thing to do is repair them as early as possible. If there are collection accounts, contact the collection agency and make arrangements to pay them. Then, make certain you got the proper documentation from the collection company indicating that the account was paid in full. When you pay those collection accounts, the reporting bureau is supposed to fix the mistake and report the correct information to the other credit bureaus.

The key phrase here is "supposed to." You'll want to follow up with the bureaus to make sure they've done their part and show the account as paid. Keep your documentation in a safe place.

Once you've taken care of your accounts by correcting any mistakes and settling with your creditors, you'll simply wait for some time to pass and reestablish credit. How can you reestablish credit if your credit has been hurt? First, make certain that whatever event caused your credit to deteriorate to begin with is fixed. Then you can take the next steps.

There are credit companies that specialize in working with those who are or have recently gone through tough times. These companies also buy information from credit-reporting bureaus to find people with hurt credit to whom they can issue a credit card. Don't be surprised when you get a credit card offer in the mail; it just may be from one of these companies.

When credit has been damaged, a lender will want to see that you can handle credit responsibly again. You do this with a new credit account. Your credit line will be small, anything from $200 to $1,000, but it will still be a credit account. Lenders typically like to see a minimum of three credit trade lines being used after bad credit has been repaired.

Take baby steps. Don't think you have to do everything at

once and just work on one account at a time. Soon, you'll find that your credit scores have improved as the negative information moves further beyond the two-year timeline.

Then concentrate on keeping your balances at 30 percent of your available credit. Even if your limit is $1,000 and not the $10,000 you had before your credit was hurt, the credit score doesn't look at how large the credit line is but how you use it.

ALTERNATIVE CREDIT

FHA and Fannie Mae accept "alternative" credit. Alternative credit accounts are accounts that are paid each month yet don't qualify as installment or revolving accounts, such as an automobile loan or a credit card.

Alternative credit accounts are utility bills such as a telephone, cable, water, or electricity. Lenders can accept these types of accounts and still approve your loan if you can document that you have paid these accounts on their due dates for the previous 12 months.

This means getting statements from your phone or cable company showing timely payments.

For lenders to use alternative credit, the accounts must be entered onto the credit report itself in addition to simply providing the documentation of timely payment.

Alternative credit is a viable, albeit time-consuming, method of getting approved for a loan. When you check your credit report and you don't have three consumer trade lines, it's possible your lender can accept alternative credit.

BANKRUPTCIES AND CREDIT

Sometimes an event happens that is so damaging to the consumer that there appears no way out. Bankruptcy laws were established many years ago to give people a fresh start.

There are two types of bankruptcies: Chapter 13 and Chapter 7. Chapter 13 is sometimes called the Wage Earner plan because the credit accounts aren't completely wiped away but paid for, bit by bit, out of the consumer's wages each pay period.

A judge will review a person's application for a Chapter 13 filing, then determine which creditors will get paid how much. Certain things such as property and income taxes and spousal and child support can't be included in a Chapter 13 bankruptcy.

Chapter 13 bankruptcies can take up to five years for creditors to be repaid. Once the repayment period has expired, the Chapter 13 is considered "discharged."

A Chapter 7 wipes out all previous dischargeable debt in one fell swoop. After all the bankruptcy filing has been signed by the judge and recorded, the Chapter 7 bankruptcy is also discharged.

Consumers must pass an income "litmus" test to see if they can qualify for the Chapter 7 discharge. To qualify for Chapter 7 the consumer must make no more than the median income for the area. Income is calculated by using the previous six months worth of total monthly income. If the consumer makes more than the median income for the area, he may not file for a Chapter 7 bankruptcy, but only for a Chapter 13.

The interesting thing about the different types of bankruptcy is how lenders view the discharge date.

A bankruptcy can appear on a credit report for seven years or more, but many don't know that you can still get a mortgage with a bankruptcy showing on a credit report. Conventional and government loans simply ask that the discharge date be at least two years old.

That means that if two years have passed since the discharge date, a lender will consider your mortgage application as long as you have reestablished credit with a minimum of three separate trade lines—regardless of the bankruptcy showing up on a credit report.

But the twist is that a Chapter 13 can be discharged only after the repayment period has elapsed. If you have a three-year repayment plan, then you may have to wait another two years for the Chapter 13 to be discharged.

Some lenders have adopted a nicer stance and review the actual filing date of the Chapter 13 instead of requiring that the Chapter 13 be discharged. If you've got either type of bankruptcy in your history and are exploring conventional financing, make sure you tell your loan officer at the very beginning.

Good news though, again, regarding FHA loans and bankruptcies: An FHA loan allows consumers to obtain a mortgage loan while still in a Chapter 13 repayment plan. As long as the loan gets a credit approval and meets the minimum credit score requirements, an FHA loan may be the way to go.

You will need to get the court's permission to buy a condo, co-op, or townhouse. The court may want to know why you're buying real estate instead of paying back your creditors. But I've never heard of a court denying such a request as long as the consumer has made timely Chapter 13 payments. That, too, is an FHA lender's requirement: You must be able to show that all of the Chapter 13 payments have been made on time.

SUBPRIME MORTGAGE LOANS

A final approach to credit and condo buying is the *subprime loan*. Subprime lending took it on the chin recently and nearly vanished from the face of the earth. But subprime lending has been around for decades, and it has a place in the credit markets when used properly.

Recall that one of the best ways to reestablish a credit score is by having a timely mortgage history. But if your credit has been damaged due to a life event such as sickness or the temporary loss of a job, and a property comes up that you must absolutely have, a subprime loan may be a good fit.

Subprime loans are for those with credit scores typically below 580. They require a bit more in down payment. Be prepared to pay 10 to 20 percent down for a subprime mortgage loan and also have higher rates. How much higher?

When you compare 30-year fixed rates for conventional and subprime loans, you may find a conventional rate at 6.50 percent and a subprime rate of 9.50 percent. The rates are higher, but then again there is a higher risk factor involved with recent credit problems.

Most subprime loans also offer a hybrid model that is lower than a fixed-rate mortgage to help ease the pain. If a subprime fixed rate is offered at 9.50 percent, then you can expect a 3/1 or 5/1 hybrid rate to be in the 8.50 percent range.

And because it is a hybrid, there is also one other important feature to consider: the fully indexed rate when the hybrid resets into an annual adjustable-rate mortgage. With subprime mortgage loans, the index can be astonishingly high, with indexes in the 8 or 9 percent range common.

If a subprime loan was based on the one-year Treasury bill and the index was at 4 percent when combined with a 9 percent margin, the rate would adjust to 13 percent! At 8.50 percent on a $300,000 loan, the payment in this instance would rise from $2,306 per month all the way to $3,318 per month!

That got a lot of people into trouble. When their loans adjusted, many of them faced foreclosure. This of course is the opposite of what a subprime mortgage loan is supposed to do, that is, get people into a mortgage loan and give them time to repair their credit.

The strategy with a subprime hybrid is to make sure you know what the payment could go to when the hybrid adjusts, and to make sure you can refinance into a conventional loan when your credit has improved.

The bugaboo with that strategy is that it assumes property values will increase—or hang steady at the very least. After all, historically, home prices rise over the years. But if property values go down and the loan value is actually higher than the property value, a lender won't make a loan on the property. Lenders require some equity in the property on any refinance.

Subprime loans do have a place—as long as you understand every detail of the loan and all possible consequences. But why bother? Why not simply wait it out, repair the credit, and apply later on? That's a good strategy, but if mortgage payments are lower than renting and you have some down payment, it's something to consider.

Once you take out a subprime loan it's critical to pay close attention to your credit accounts and pay them on time, every time. One late mortgage payment on a subprime loan and your score could drop below where it was when you took out the initial subprime mortgage!

Where do you find subprime mortgages? It used to be that they could be found nearly anywhere, with all banks great and small offering loan programs for those with damaged credit. With the recent mortgage debacle, they have all but vanished. They are still around, but just a handful of lenders still offer them and their guidelines have been tightened.

| CHAPTER 7 |

Closing Costs: What They Are and How to Negotiate Them

SOME CALL CLOSING COSTS an inherent evil. I don't know whether they are evil, but I do know that closing costs are something you need to consider when you think about saving money to buy real estate. Although coming up with the down payment is understandably at the top of buyers' minds, they shouldn't forget about the money they will need for closing costs.

Closing costs pay for services of third parties who directly or indirectly participate in the sales process. To understand these closing costs, let's first review who these people are, what they do, and how much they charge for their services. There are required services and optional services. The following are required services:

> Appraisal
> Credit Report

- Application Fee
- Tax Service
- Flood Certificate
- Lender Fees
- Mortgage Broker Fees
- Settlement or Closing Fee
- Title Insurance
- Document Fees
- HOA Fees
- Attorney Fees
- Courier Fees
- Government Fees

APPRAISAL

The appraisal, performed by an individual appraiser, is a report that attempts to determine current *market value* by comparing the sales price of the property with recent sales of other units in your project or ones nearby.

An appraiser will review the sales contract on the property, note how many bedrooms the unit has, how many square feet there are, and so on; then he'll search public records and the *multiple-listing service*, or MLS, for sales of similar size and features.

The condo appraisal will also review information similar to what a lender will address regarding the number of units, how many are rented out, amount of commercial space, and so on.

Condos are relatively easier to appraise than single-family homes. Single-family, detached homes—especially in suburban areas—are rarely exactly alike in terms of square footage and design. Not so for projects, where most of the units are built exactly alike. Generally speaking, whether it has one, two, or three bedrooms, a condo, co-op, or townhouse usually has the same basic design as other units in the project. (One exception: High-rise condos will typically have their premium units at or near the very top of the building.)

It's easy to determine if the sales price of the unit meets current market activity by comparing the sales price of units that have sold in the most recent 12-month period. An appraiser will be required to find at minimum three *comparable sales*— called "comps"—in the complex, and typically one unit outside the project but nearby.

The lender will review the appraisal before making any loan decision. That's to make certain the property is marketable, that is, that in an open market the unit could sell in a reasonable period of time for at least the current purchase price.

In a balanced market, the appraised value will typically come in at the sales price. When Realtors do their market analysis at the very beginning, they can determine the price at which the unit should sell based on the sales price of other units in the project.

Sometimes, though, in a softer market, the appraisal will come in below the sales price. That means other units in the project have sold for less than the sales price.

When a unit comes in lower than the sales price, the buyer has a decision to make; do I continue with this purchase, or not? Lenders base mortgage loans on the lower of the sales price or appraised value and can have an effect on how much money you'll need to come up with at the closing table.

For instance, a property sells for $300,000, the appraisal comes in at $290,000, and you had planned on putting 10 percent down. Because the appraisal came in low, the lender will use the $290,000 as the loan basis.

You will first pay for the difference in values, or $10,000, then factor in your 10 percent down payment on $290,000, or $29,000. With a $300,000 sales price you would need to pay 10 percent of $300,000, or $30,000. In this example, you would need to come in with $39,000.

If this happens to you, you're not stuck. Sales contracts typically have language built in that protects you, essentially saying, "If the appraisal comes back lower than the sales price the deal's off and the buyer gets his earnest money back."

Then the seller regroups and rethinks the sales price. If the appraised value is, in fact, valid and substantiated by comps in the project, then it's hard to hold on to the original selling price. This instance is not very common but can be seen with more frequency in depressed areas where values are falling.

Even though you pay for an appraisal, it doesn't belong to you. The appraisal will be performed on behalf of the lender. It is part of your loan package, and you do have a right to receive a copy of the appraisal when it's completed and paid for.

Appraisals can cost anywhere from $350 to $600. For properties that sell for more than $650,000, expect to pay $450 to $600. For units that sell for $1 million and up, the lender may require two appraisals.

CREDIT REPORT

A lender will also run a credit report on you after you complete the loan application and have signed the required forms authorizing the lender to do so. A credit report is good for 90 days, after which an update will be performed at an additional cost.

Sometimes a credit report that is pulled on two people at the same time shows one person with good credit and one person with not so good credit. If the loan is being denied because of the not so good credit, then a report will be ordered by the lender and *reissued,* removing the person with bad credit from the credit report.

In community property states, the lender will still require the credit report on the person with bad credit, but only to see if there are any joint credit accounts for which the buyer will be responsible.

Credit reports typically run between $15 and $20. Updates can cost $5 or so.

APPLICATION FEE

Sometimes an *application fee* is collected up front by the lender. This fee covers the costs of the appraisal and credit reports. It may also offset any initial overhead the mortgage company acquires during the approval process.

An application fee is also inconvenient if you get upset with the lender and want to transfer your appraisal to another mortgage company. When you pay an application fee you technically haven't paid for the appraisal, and if the mortgage company gets upset with you as well, it just might not release the appraisal because, well, you didn't pay for it; you only paid an application fee.

For your own protection, even though you may write a check for an application fee, simply putting the word "appraisal" in the memo line on the check will take care of any confusion down the road.

Application fees also let lenders know that they've got a serious client on the other end of the phone and not a "rate shopper" who will not commit until they've nearly run out of time.

Application fees can run anywhere from $300 to $500.

TAX SERVICE

A *tax service* company gets paid to research the current amount of property taxes that are due, if any, and what the taxes are on the unit itself.

A tax service company also insures a lender throughout the life of a mortgage that property taxes have been paid and are not delinquent, forcing a potential tax sale. Tax service companies let a lender know when taxes become seriously past due so the lender can take action. For example, the lender can pay the taxes on your behalf, then schedule a repayment plan for you to pay it back.

Tax service companies typically charge $15 to $25 for this service that you pay for at closing.

FLOOD CERTIFICATE

A *flood certificate* researches recent Federal Emergency Management Association (FEMA) flood charts to see if any part of the structure or grounds is in a flood zone. Every decade, FEMA surveys an area and provides an updated flood plain map, and flood reporting companies provide the data to the lender.

Flood certificates can cost between $60 and $70.

LENDER FEES

Lender fees go by various names. Lenders may charge whatever they want, as long as they're competitive with other lenders in the area.

Except for an application fee, lender fees are paid at closing. Common lender fees include the underwriting fee, administrative fee, loan processing fee, document fee, and others.

Some of these fees are legitimate. Others are questionable. Processing a loan is a physical act. There is a *loan processor*, and it requires a lot of work to get your loan from the application stage to the closing table.

Underwriting is also a physical act. It ensures that the loan complies with lending guidelines in terms of credit, income, assets, and other loan approval requirements.

Pretty much anything else should be called a "junk" fee. Junk fees have important sounding names, but they are a bit nebulous. Common junk fees are administrative, preparation, or simply mortgage broker fees.

These fees are income to the lender. They may be used to offset a lower rate quote, or they may be pure profit.

Underwriting fees are around $500; processing fees are usually $400 to $500. Junk fees are usually no more than $400 per line item.

MORTGAGE BROKER FEES

In addition to lender charges, mortgage brokers may also charge their own fees. Most common is an *origination charge*, normally 1 percent of the loan amount. It may show up on your *settlement statement* as a "Mortgage Broker Fee" when you go to closing.

SETTLEMENT OR CLOSING FEE

Someone will oversee your closing. Who that party is depends on where you live. It could be an attorney or an escrow officer. Sometimes it's a closing agent.

The *closer* makes sure the documents are signed properly; He collects funds from the lender and disburses them to the sellers, the agents, and all the various companies involved with the closing.

When lenders send out closing papers for the buyers to sign, they do so electronically. The closer will receive and print the documents, then follow a list of official "Lenders

Instructions" that delineate exactly what is required by the buyers before the lender will send the money over for the closing.

Common lenders instructions would be:

Borrower to Sign Page 4 of the Loan Application

Borrower to Sign Name Affidavit

Borrower to Provide Two Forms of Photo ID

And so on. After the closing agent does all the lender asks for, the closing agent will fax the required documents back to the lender who will make sure the closer did what he was supposed to do. Then, if everything is correct (and everything usually is), the lender sends the closer a "secret code" that will unlock the funds previously wired to the closer.

The closer will take those funds and disburse them to the appropriate parties—the inspector, the seller, the surveyor, and so on.

Closing fees can range from $300 to $500.

TITLE INSURANCE

Title insurance is an insurance policy that protects the buyer and lender from defects on the title report. The title report is a document that shows the history of owners of the property and who sold to whom and when.

A "clean" title report means that there are no previous claims to the unit from previous owners or heirs and that the property is free of judgments and liens. Individuals and even legal organizations may have an ownership interest in a property without being on a mortgage.

Title insurance protects the lender and the buyer by ensuring that there are no previous claims or liens.

How could a previous claim exist? There are, in fact, many ways. A husband and wife get divorced and one of the "exes" never signs any documentation releasing his claim on the house, even though in the divorce decree it says he does.

A contractor could have done some work on the property and was never paid or paid satisfactorily. There could be a lawsuit filed and a judgment filed on the unit.

Even some long-lost heir from three or four owners back could pop up and make a claim against the estate. "I'm the grandson of one of the previous owners and it says in this will that I own this house. Now get out!"

Title insurance varies wildly by state and by the type of policies offered. Some policies are as high as 1 percent of the loan amount and as low as a few hundred dollars.

DOCUMENT FEES

This is a common fee charged by an attorney who reviews the loan documents or it could be from the closing agent who prepares the legal documents for closing. Whoever is responsible for ensuring that the closing papers are legal will typically charge a document fee.

In Texas, for instance, an attorney must review all loan

papers. The attorney will then warrant them. In other states, a closing agent or the lender can provide the same guarantee that the loan papers meet lending guidelines.

Document fees can range from $200 to $400 per set of documents.

HOA FEES

This is (typically) a monthly fee paid to the HOA that cover a variety of things including helping to pay for project insurance premiums, maintenance in the compound, and management.

The more amenities a condo or co-op offers, the more you can expect to pay in HOA fees. Typical HOA fees run around $200 per month, but they can go much higher.

ATTORNEY FEES

Again, this will vary depending on locale. In Illinois, for instance, an attorney holds the closing for the buyer and the seller—and can issue title insurance. In Texas, a licensed attorney must review all mortgage loans. In California, there is no requirement for an attorney at all. When I was a mortgage broker in San Diego, I never met an attorney or saw one involved in a transaction other than representing the estate of someone who was deceased.

Attorney fees, when applicable, range from $100 to $500 per transaction.

COURIER FEES

This is a fee charged by a courier service or overnight delivery service to deliver signed loan documents from the closing agent to the lender. This can literally be a driver—even a bicyclist in some cities—who picks up the loan papers from the attorney's office and delivers them to the lender.

Courier charges are nominal, $25 or so.

GOVERNMENT FEES

The county and state governments will also get their share of money, typically in the way of fees to record the transaction in the public record or (to a greater extent) in the form of taxes.

Government fees and taxes are simply too numerous to mention. The rules change not only from state to state, but often from county to county!

There is a second type of service, called a nonrequired service, which includes pest inspection (some states require this), property inspection, and home warranty.

Some states actually do require a pest inspection for infestation of termites or other wood-eating insects. But most condominiums and co-ops will be attached to one another, so few lenders will require a termite report.

Some buyers simply want to have the peace of mind that their new home is free from mice, rodents, or other nasty little creatures. Pest inspections typically cost around $100.

At first glance, a property inspection sounds like an appraisal: Someone goes out and inspects the property and gives it a value. But the property inspector actually checks to make sure everything is in good working order.

Property inspections are optional, but I cannot understand why anyone wouldn't want to have their prospective purchase inspected from top to bottom by an independent party who will document any deficiencies or defects.

The property inspector will switch the lights on and off and check the disposal, plumbing, and electrical outlets. In the case of a townhouse, he'll even crawl through an attic, checking on insulation and air conditioning and heating units.

After a thorough inspection, the inspector will issue a report showing what he checked, if it works, if it doesn't, or if it needs repair. Inspections will also note what type of repair is needed that is critical (hot water heater not up to code) or not.

Inspections can range from $200 to $400 per job.

A home warranty is also a neat little idea that typically guarantees any appliances that are included with the home sale will be replaced within a one- or two-year period if they fail. Most often it's the seller of the property who offers a home warranty as part of his or her listing agreement.

If, for instance, a trash compactor goes out in the first year, the owner would call the warranty company, who would make arrangements for a new trash compactor to be delivered for a nominal fee.

I recall when my trash compactor went out after about six months of owning a new home. Instead of shelling out a couple hundred dollars for a new compactor, I paid just a $35 fee to have it delivered and installed. The same thing happened with my garbage disposal. The seller paid for the warranty, and I got some brand-new appliances out of the deal at little cost to me.

PREPAID AND NONPREPAID ITEMS

So far, we've discussed one-time charges you may incur when buying your condo, co-op, or townhouse, but there will also be costs you'll see over and over again that you'll need to know about. They are called "prepaid" charges.

Closing costs are divided into two categories: *prepaid* or *nonprepaid*, sometimes called "recurring" and "nonrecurring" fees, respectively.

Nonrecurring, or nonprepaid, fees are the one-time costs for an appraisal or attorney. Recurring, or prepaid, costs are things such as property taxes, insurance, and even interest that is prepaid when you go to the closing.

You will continue to pay these fees over and over again for as long as you own the property. If you have escrow or *impound accounts*—where you pay a portion of your annual tax bill each month so that you'll have automatically paid your taxes by the time they come due—you'll need to set those up when you go to closing. Your lender will collect three months worth of property taxes at closing to set up the *escrow account*. The two extra months worth of taxes are a reserve just in case property values increase and your tax bill at the end of the year is higher than anticipated.

If your annual property tax bill is $1,200, that means one

month's taxes equals $100. Three months of taxes to establish an escrow account means you will be coming to the closing table with $300, in addition to the nonprepaid items mentioned earlier.

Finally, *prepaid interest* will be collected at your closing. Prepaid interest is determined by the number of days up to the following month multiplied by the daily interest that accrues.

For instance, if you close on the 20th of the month, the lender will collect interest from the 20th to the 30th (or 31st). This acts as your first mortgage payment; you're just paying it early.

Mortgage interest is paid in arrears, which means that each time you make a mortgage payment on the first of each month you're paying for the number of days you owned the property in the previous month. It's the opposite of rent, which you pay ahead of time.

Some people may tell you to close toward the end of the month because it saves you money. They're talking about accrual of interest. If you closed on the last day of the month you would only need to bring in one day's worth of interest instead of 10 days worth, had you closed on the 20th.

GOOD-FAITH ESTIMATE

So who wants to pay all those closing costs, anyway? Who needs an attorney or a processing fee? After all, you're in command, right?

The fact is that some closing costs can be negotiated down

or even eliminated altogether while other closing fees are non-negotiable.

When you apply for a mortgage with a lender or you get a rate quote, you'll typically ask for their *good-faith estimate* of closing charges, or simply the "Good Faith."

By law, a loan officer is required to give you this Good Faith immediately when you take a loan application face to face or within three business days of receiving a loan application online, by mail, or by fax.

The Good Faith is a form that attempts to disclose to you, all in good faith, the possible costs you'll encounter when you go to closing. Sounds fair enough, but beware: Some loan officers will manipulate the Good Faith and try to trick you into using them instead of their competition.

The Good Faith is divided into different sections and line-itemed from top to bottom beginning with item number 801, reserved for an origination charge, all the way through to item 1320, for a pest inspection. The form can be intimidating at first glance. But if you look at it in sections, it becomes a tad more readable.

The first section (the "800" section) is reserved for items payable in conjunction with the mortgage—things such as appraisals, points, credit report, tax service, processing fees, origination charges, and so on.

Section 1100 (I know it's not directly after 800 numerically but it is indeed the second section on the Good Faith) includes all title and title-related charges, such as escrow or closing fees, attorney fees, and document preparation charges.

Section 1200 is reserved for government recording and transfer charges and tax stamps.

Section 1300 is essentially anything that doesn't fit into the listed categories so far and would include things such as pest and property inspections. Surveys would also belong here.

These sections are nonrecurring items, meaning they are one-time charges. This is compared to recurring items or prepaid items, meaning charges that will occur again in the future. These charges come next with the 900 series; this is the area where property taxes, mortgage insurance, and interest charges will be listed. Finally, section 1000 lists items for any escrow or impound accounts that need to be established.

At the very end of the form it says, "Total Estimated Settlement Charges." Prepaid and nonprepaid items are subtotaled and totaled.

Most people's eyes go straight toward the last line. Unfortunately they don't read the entire document or take note of the different service providers.

Even if you do review the entire document, remember, this estimate comes from a loan officer from a mortgage company, not from your attorney's office or the title agency.

A loan officer can only control her own closing costs, not those of third parties. She can only provide an estimate. A sneaky loan officer can trick you into thinking you're getting a great deal by low-balling third-party estimates.

Here's an example of how a loan officer can make her estimate appear better than her competition by manipulating third-party charges.

	Lender A	Lender B
Appraisal	$ 350	$ 350
Credit Report	$ 20	$ 20
Points	$2,000	$3,000
Processing	$ 400	$ 400
Total	$2,770	$3,770

So far, Lender B (with the sneaky loan officer) appears higher because he's charging $1,000 more in points. But now let's review some other charges on the Good Faith:

	Lender A	Lender B
Escrow	$ 300	$ 100
Attorney	$ 500	$ 100
Title Insurance	$ 800	$ 175
Survey	$ 450	$ 200
Documents	$ 200	$ 50
Total	$2,250	$ 425
Grand Total	$5,020	$4,195

Lender A looks more expensive by $825, so it's a no-brainer, right? Wrong. Lender B intentionally low-balled the nonlender charges while increasing her own.

Next stop: your closing. You arrive at the settlement table and the first thing you'll see is the final settlement statement with everyone's charges on them. Closers make sure this is the first document you'll review because it's usually the one that causes problems.

But you notice something: While Lender B's lender charges

were in line, the nonlender charges add up to $2,250 and not $425! So you call the sneaky loan officer from your cell phone and demand to know what's up.

"Sorry," the loan officer replies, "I don't have any control over attorney or escrow charges. They are what they are. It says right there on the sheet that those are only estimates."

Do you walk away from the table and risk losing the property and your earnest money deposit, or do you grit your teeth and sign your papers? I thought so. And as you sign, you vow never to refer the loan officer to anyone. Not that she would care. Loan officers like that don't stay in business for very long.

USING THE ANNUAL PERCENTAGE RATE TO COMPARE LENDERS

When you get your initial rate and fee quotes from your loan officer, you may be confused by the *annual percentage rate*, or APR. In fact, many loan officers dismiss the APR altogether, calling it misleading and hard to understand. I disagree. The APR is a tool to compare lenders. But it cannot be discussed meaningfully without a thorough explanation of closing costs and their relation to the interest rate attached to the note. That's why we're explaining it in this chapter. But it should be used as an adjunct to the sections in chapter 3 on finding the best lender.

The APR is the cost of money borrowed, expressed as an annual rate. The APR number is an interest rate that takes into account your note rate on your quoted mortgage plus additional lender fees such as discount points, origination fees, and underwriting charges required to get the mortgage.

The APR takes into account these different fees and works out an interest rate. It is designed to provide an immediate comparison between two or more lenders. In the previous example, because Lender B had more loan charges (points), the APR would be higher, even though the note rate was the same.

Lender A quoted 6 percent with $2,000 in points and Lender B quoted 6 percent with $3,000 in points. Because of the different lender charges, Lender B's APR would be higher, indicating the lender charged more in fees.

Let's review the APR for this same example on a $200,000 mortgage and a 30-year fixed-rate loan.

Appraisal	$ 350	$ 350
Credit Report	$ 20	$ 20
Points	$2,000	$3,000
Processing	$ 400	$ 400
Total	$2,770	$3,770
Note Rate	6.00%	6.00%
APR	6.13%	6.18%

Lender B's APR is higher than Lender A's and shows that Lender B is charging more in fees.

Used properly, the APR shows who has the best deal. But you must take certain precautions because that number, too, can be manipulated.

To properly compare APRs, make sure your note rates are exactly the same on the very same loan program. APR comparisons won't work very well if note rates are different. Second, make sure the loan officer doesn't include any prepaid interest charges.

Prepaid (per diem) interest is a factor when calculating APR. As you may recall, prepaid interest will be lower if you close at the end of the month and higher if you close toward the first of the month.

If you know you're closing on the 20th, make sure that all lender quotes include the exact same number of days of prepaid interest in their calculations. For best results, have them calculate the APR with zero days of prepaid interest charges.

Because APR comparisons only work when the loan terms are the same, you can't compare a fixed rate with an adjustable rate or a hybrid. And comparing different loan terms won't work either.

But the APR is a good, quick way to tell who might be loading up on lender fees—as long as you're comparing the exact same loan terms and note rate.

Another easy way to compare good-faith estimates: Simply disregard nonlender charges altogether. This is what I call "comparing the 800 series."

Because the 800 series are the only charges the loan officer can accurately quote, comparing nonlender charges on the good-faith estimate is a waste of time.

Loan officers have a fairly good grip on closing costs. But a mortgage broker may not know exactly who the lender will ultimately be. Wholesale lenders who work with mortgage brokers have different fees.

NEGOTIATING CLOSING COSTS

Are any of these costs negotiable? There are a lot of fees from a lot of different sources; surely some of them aren't etched in stone, right? Right! Some of them are negotiable, but most of the negotiable ones are from the lender and lender-related charges.

➤ *Appraisal.* Typically not negotiable under most circumstances. It's the lender who orders an appraisal, not the consumer. However, there are different types of appraisals, and loans that have both good credit and a sizable down payment (20 percent or more) may be able to obtain a "property inspection waiver" or a "drive-by" appraisal. A property inspection waiver means the property doesn't need to be appraised at all (only public records will be reviewed). A property inspection waiver may only cost $50 or so, whereas a drive-by appraisal, one where the appraiser only verifies the property's existence and takes pictures from the outside, may cost only $175 or so.

➤ *Credit Report.* Again, the lender, not the consumer, orders credit reports. But it should be noted that any charge from a third party cannot be "padded" by the lender or any other agents. For instance, if your credit report costs $20 from the credit reporting agency, the lender can't charge you $25 and pocket the difference. Lenders are required to keep third-party invoices on file forever in case of an audit.

➤ *Application Fee.* Yes, negotiable. In fact, you may be able to negotiate it out of existence! But remember, just because a fee is negotiable doesn't mean the other party will agree to your wishes.

➤ *Tax Service.* Not negotiable; again, ordered by the lender.

➤ *Flood Certificate.* Not negotiable; ordered by the lender.

➤ *Lender Fees.* Negotiable. All lender fees are up for grabs, but I believe that from a mortgage company's point of view there are two types of fees: those that are "required" and those that "would be nice to have."

A mortgage company may have a $300 processing fee and a $500 underwriting fee. Sometimes loan officers have the leverage to "waive" a fee on behalf of the company if it means getting the mortgage loan in the door. But other fees are required, and if the loan officer waives a required fee, the lender will take a $500 required fee out of the loan officer's paycheck.

➤ *Mortgage Broker Fees.* Negotiable. When you first begin shopping for interest rates, you must also shop for the fees the mortgage broker or mortgage company charges. As seen in the previous example, you could get the very same rate quote but with different lender charges.

➤ *Settlement* or *Closing Fee.* Not negotiable.

➤ *Title Insurance.* Not negotiable.

➤ *Document Fees.* Not negotiable.

> ➤ *HOA Fees.* Not negotiable.

> ➤ *Attorney Fees.* Not negotiable.

> ➤ *Courier Fees.* Not negotiable.

> ➤ *Government Fees.* Not negotiable.

FEES AND REFINANCING

Yes, there will be closing costs if you ever decide to refinance your loan—pretty much the same costs as when you purchased the property. But there are ways to save on some of the costs.

> ➤ *Appraisal.* If you're thinking of refinancing, call your old appraisal company. Tell them you'll request their services in exchange for a discount.

> ➤ *Attorney Fees.* Depending on the services attorneys provide where you live, you may also want to contact the one you used when you purchased the property. Tell them you're thinking of refinancing and make the same offer that you made the appraiser.

> ➤ *Lender* and *Mortgage Broker Fees.* Here's a good tactic to use when you make the original purchase. If a loan officer isn't budging on, say, waiving a fee, before you give in ask, "What if I were to use your services again, if I ever refinance. Would you waive *that* fee?" If they agree, get it in writing so you can remind them of their promise when you come back.

➤ *Title Insurance.* Title insurance discounts vary. Again, when you make the initial purchase, ask about a discount "reissue" rate for using them again in the future if you refinance. Some states require you use the same title company and others issue a discount based upon the age of the current policy.

Some companies own both a title company and a closing company; if you use both of their services you can get discounts on title insurance and closing costs.

NO–CLOSING COST MORTGAGE

You've seen the ads or heard them on the radio or Internet, "No closing costs!" What a deal, right? Why doesn't every lender offer them and why would people even consider paying closing costs if they didn't have to?

In reality, every lender or mortgage company offers a no–closing cost loan. It's simply a mortgage loan that has the interest rate adjusted to offset some or all of the closing fees. It works like this:

Say there is a mortgage loan at $500,000. On a regular 30-year fixed rate at 6.50 percent with typical closing costs, the monthly payment works out to $3,160—with around $3,500 of nonrecurring fees and $2,000 worth of prepaids.

As discussed in chapter 3, you can typically "buy down" an interest rate by $1/4$ percent for each discount point you pay. In this case if you paid a point, the rate would drop to 6.25 percent, the payment would drop slightly to $3,078 per month, and you added $5,000 to your closing charges.

Conversely, you can increase your interest rate by $1/4$ percent from 6.50 percent to 6.75 percent and the monthly payment goes up to $3,242 per month. Just as you can decrease your rate by paying a point, you can increase your rate by $1/4$ percent and the lender gives you a one-point credit, or in this instance $5,000 to cover closing costs.

Your closing costs added up to $5,500 and your lender gave you a credit in exchange for a higher rate, but now you only have $500 in closing costs and not $5,500!

There actually is no such thing as a no–closing cost loan. There may not appear to be closing costs, but there are higher monthly payments. In this example, your payment would go up by $82.

How do you evaluate a no–closing cost loan to see if it's right for you? Take the monthly increase in payment and divide that amount into the money you saved in closing costs, or in this case $5,000: $5,000 divided by $82 is 60.98, or 61 months.

Be careful of no–closing cost ads; sometimes in the fine print it will read "no lender closing costs" rather than "no closing costs whatsoever."

Closing costs and interest rates are the single biggest shell game in the business. But because you read this book, you won't get taken in!

Monthly Payment Schedules

The following schedule shows monthly payments per thousand dollars financed. To calculate your monthly payment:

1. Find your interest rate in the first column.
2. Move across to the appropriate column for your term.
3. Multiply that number by the number of thousand dollars financed.

EXAMPLE

If you are borrowing $150,000 at 6.50 percent interest for a 30-year term:

$6.32 x 150 (thousands)—$948.00 principal and interest payment

Thus, your monthly payment for both principal and interest is $948.

Rate	40 years	30 years	25 years	20 years	15 years	10 years
2.500	$3.30	$3.95	$4.49	$5.30	$6.67	$ 9.43
2.625	$3.37	$4.02	$4.55	$5.36	$6.73	$ 9.48
2.750	$3.44	$4.08	$4.61	$5.42	$6.79	$ 9.54
2.875	$3.51	$4.15	$4.68	$5.48	$6.85	$ 9.60
3.000	$3.58	$4.22	$4.74	$5.55	$6.91	$ 9.66
3.125	$3.65	$4.28	$4.81	$5.61	$6.97	$ 9.71
3.250	$3.73	$4.35	$4.87	$5.67	$7.03	$ 9.77
3.375	$3.80	$4.42	$4.94	$5.74	$7.09	$ 9.83
3.500	$3.87	$4.49	$5.01	$5.80	$7.15	$ 9.89
3.625	$3.95	$4.56	$5.07	$5.86	$7.21	$ 9.95
3.750	$4.03	$4.63	$5.14	$5.93	$7.27	$10.01
3.875	$4.10	$4.70	$5.21	$5.99	$7.33	$10.07
4.000	$4.18	$4.77	$5.28	$6.06	$7.40	$10.12
4.125	$4.26	$4.85	$5.35	$6.13	$7.46	$10.18
4.250	$4.34	$4.92	$5.42	$6.19	$7.52	$10.24
4.375	$4.42	$4.99	$5.49	$6.26	$7.59	$10.30
4.500	$4.50	$5.07	$5.56	$6.33	$7.65	$10.36
4.625	$4.58	$5.14	$5.63	$6.39	$7.71	$10.42
4.750	$4.66	$5.22	$5.70	$6.46	$7.78	$10.48
4.875	$4.74	$5.29	$5.77	$6.53	$7.84	$10.55
5.000	$4.82	$5.37	$5.85	$6.60	$7.91	$10.61
5.125	$4.91	$5.44	$5.92	$6.67	$7.97	$10.67
5.250	$4.99	$5.52	$5.99	$6.74	$8.04	$10.73
5.375	$5.07	$5.60	$6.07	$6.81	$8.10	$10.79
5.500	$5.16	$5.68	$6.14	$6.88	$8.17	$10.85
5.625	$5.24	$5.76	$6.22	$6.95	$8.24	$10.91

Rate	40 years	30 years	25 years	20 years	15 years	10 years
5.750	$5.33	$5.84	$6.29	$7.02	$ 8.30	$10.98
5.875	$5.42	$5.92	$6.37	$7.09	$ 8.37	$11.04
6.000	$5.50	$6.00	$6.44	$7.16	$ 8.44	$11.10
6.125	$5.59	$6.08	$6.52	$7.24	$ 8.51	$11.16
6.250	$5.68	$6.16	$6.60	$7.31	$ 8.57	$11.23
6.375	$5.77	$6.24	$6.67	$7.38	$ 8.64	$11.29
6.500	$5.85	$6.32	$6.75	$7.46	$ 8.71	$11.35
6.625	$5.94	$6.40	$6.83	$7.53	$ 8.78	$11.42
6.750	$6.03	$6.49	$6.91	$7.60	$ 8.85	$11.48
6.875	$6.12	$6.57	$6.99	$7.68	$ 8.92	$11.55
7.000	$6.21	$6.65	$7.07	$7.75	$ 8.99	$11.61
7.125	$6.31	$6.74	$7.15	$7.83	$ 9.06	$11.68
7.250	$6.40	$6.82	$7.23	$7.90	$ 9.13	$11.74
7.375	$6.49	$6.91	$7.31	$7.98	$ 9.20	$11.81
7.500	$6.58	$6.99	$7.39	$8.06	$ 9.27	$11.87
7.625	$6.67	$7.08	$7.47	$8.13	$ 9.34	$11.94
7.750	$6.77	$7.16	$7.55	$8.21	$ 9.41	$12.00
7.875	$6.86	$7.25	$7.64	$8.29	$ 9.48	$12.07
8.000	$6.95	$7.34	$7.72	$8.36	$ 9.56	$12.13
8.125	$7.05	$7.42	$7.80	$8.44	$ 9.63	$12.20
8.250	$7.14	$7.51	$7.88	$8.52	$ 9.70	$12.27
8.375	$7.24	$7.60	$7.97	$8.60	$ 9.77	$12.33
8.500	$7.33	$7.69	$8.05	$8.68	$ 9.85	$12.40
8.625	$7.43	$7.78	$8.14	$8.76	$ 9.92	$12.47
8.750	$7.52	$7.87	$8.22	$8.84	$ 9.99	$12.53
8.875	$7.62	$7.96	$8.31	$8.92	$10.07	$12.60
9.000	$7.71	$8.05	$8.39	$9.00	$10.14	$12.67
9.125	$7.81	$8.14	$8.48	$9.08	$10.22	$12.74
9.250	$7.91	$8.23	$8.56	$9.16	$10.29	$12.80

Rate	40 years	30 years	25 years	20 years	15 years	10 years
9.375	$ 8.00	$ 8.32	$ 8.65	$ 9.24	$10.37	$12.87
9.500	$ 8.10	$ 8.41	$ 8.74	$ 9.32	$10.44	$12.94
9.625	$ 8.20	$ 8.50	$ 8.82	$ 9.40	$10.52	$13.01
9.750	$ 8.30	$ 8.59	$ 8.91	$ 9.49	$10.59	$13.08
9.875	$ 8.39	$ 8.68	$ 9.00	$ 9.57	$10.67	$13.15
10.000	$ 8.49	$ 8.78	$ 9.09	$ 9.65	$10.75	$13.22
10.125	$ 8.59	$ 8.87	$ 9.18	$ 9.73	$10.82	$13.28
10.250	$ 8.69	$ 8.96	$ 9.26	$ 9.82	$10.90	$13.35
10.375	$ 8.79	$ 9.05	$ 9.35	$ 9.90	$10.98	$13.42
10.500	$ 8.89	$ 9.15	$ 9.44	$ 9.98	$11.05	$13.49
10.625	$ 8.98	$ 9.24	$ 9.53	$10.07	$11.13	$13.56
10.750	$ 9.08	$ 9.33	$ 9.62	$10.15	$11.21	$13.63
10.875	$ 9.18	$ 9.43	$ 9.71	$10.24	$11.29	$13.70
11.000	$ 9.28	$ 9.52	$ 9.80	$10.32	$11.37	$13.78
11.125	$ 9.38	$ 9.62	$ 9.89	$10.41	$11.44	$13.85
11.250	$ 9.48	$ 9.71	$ 9.98	$10.49	$11.52	$13.92
11.375	$ 9.58	$ 9.81	$10.07	$10.58	$11.60	$13.99
11.500	$ 9.68	$ 9.90	$10.16	$10.66	$11.68	$14.06
11.625	$ 9.78	$10.00	$10.26	$10.75	$11.76	$14.13
11.750	$ 9.88	$10.09	$10.35	$10.84	$11.84	$14.20
11.875	$ 9.98	$10.19	$10.44	$10.92	$11.92	$14.27
12.000	$10.08	$10.29	$10.53	$11.01	$12.00	$14.35
12.125	$10.19	$10.38	$10.62	$11.10	$12.08	$14.42
12.250	$10.29	$10.48	$10.72	$11.19	$12.16	$14.49
12.375	$10.39	$10.58	$10.81	$11.27	$12.24	$14.56
12.500	$10.49	$10.67	$10.90	$11.36	$12.33	$14.64
12.625	$10.59	$10.77	$11.00	$11.45	$12.41	$14.71
12.750	$10.69	$10.87	$11.09	$11.54	$12.49	$14.78
12.875	$10.79	$10.96	$11.18	$11.63	$12.57	$14.86

Rate	40 years	30 years	25 years	20 years	15 years	10 years
13.000	$10.90	$11.06	$11.28	$11.72	$12.65	$14.93
13.125	$11.00	$11.16	$11.37	$11.80	$12.73	$15.00
13.250	$11.10	$11.26	$11.47	$11.89	$12.82	$15.08
13.375	$11.20	$11.36	$11.56	$11.98	$12.90	$15.15
13.500	$11.30	$11.45	$11.66	$12.07	$12.98	$15.23
13.625	$11.40	$11.55	$11.75	$12.16	$13.07	$15.30
13.750	$11.51	$11.65	$11.85	$12.25	$13.15	$15.38
13.875	$11.61	$11.75	$11.94	$12.34	$13.23	$15.45
14.000	$11.71	$11.85	$12.04	$12.44	$13.32	$15.53
14.125	$11.81	$11.95	$12.13	$12.53	$13.40	$15.60
14.250	$11.92	$12.05	$12.23	$12.62	$13.49	$15.68
14.375	$12.02	$12.15	$12.33	$12.71	$13.57	$15.75
14.500	$12.12	$12.25	$12.42	$12.80	$13.66	$15.83
14.625	$12.22	$12.35	$12.52	$12.89	$13.74	$15.90
14.750	$12.33	$12.44	$12.61	$12.98	$13.83	$15.9
14.875	$12.43	$12.54	$12.71	$13.08	$13.91	$16.06
15.000	$12.53	$12.64	$12.81	$13.17	$14.00	$16.13
15.125	$12.64	$12.74	$12.91	$13.26	$14.08	$16.21
15.250	$12.74	$12.84	$13.00	$13.35	$14.17	$16.29
15.375	$12.84	$12.94	$13.10	$13.45	$14.25	$16.36
15.500	$12.94	$13.05	$13.20	$13.54	$14.34	$16.44
15.625	$13.05	$13.15	$13.30	$13.63	$14.43	$16.52
15.750	$13.15	$13.25	$13.39	$13.73	$14.51	$16.60
15.875	$13.25	$13.35	$13.49	$13.82	$14.60	$16.67
16.000	$13.36	$13.45	$13.59	$13.91	$14.69	$16.75
16.125	$13.46	$13.55	$13.69	$14.01	$14.77	$16.83
16.250	$13.56	$13.65	$13.79	$14.10	$14.86	$16.91
16.375	$13.67	$13.75	$13.88	$14.19	$14.95	$16.99
16.500	$13.77	$13.85	$13.98	$14.29	$15.04	$17.06

Rate	40 years	30 years	25 years	20 years	15 years	10 years
16.625	$13.87	$13.95	$14.08	$14.38	$15.13	$17.14
16.750	$13.98	$14.05	$14.18	$14.48	$15.21	$17.22
16.875	$14.08	$14.16	$14.28	$14.57	$15.30	$17.30
17.000	$14.18	$14.26	$14.38	$14.67	$15.39	$17.38
17.125	$14.29	$14.36	$14.48	$14.76	$15.48	$17.46
17.250	$14.39	$14.46	$14.58	$14.86	$15.57	$17.54
17.375	$14.49	$14.56	$14.68	$14.95	$15.66	$17.62
17.500	$14.60	$14.66	$14.78	$15.05	$15.75	$17.70
17.625	$14.70	$14.77	$14.87	$15.15	$15.84	$17.78
17.750	$14.80	$14.87	$14.97	$15.24	$15.92	$17.86
17.875	$14.91	$14.97	$15.07	$15.34	$16.01	$17.94
18.000	$15.01	$15.07	$15.17	$15.43	$16.10	$18.02

| G L O S S A R Y |

Abstract of Title A written record of the historical ownership of the property that helps to determine whether the property can in fact be transferred from one party to another without any previous claims. An abstract of title is used in certain parts of the country when determining if there are any previous claims on the subject property in question.

Acceleration A loan accelerates when it is paid off early, usually at the request or demand of the lender. An acceleration clause within a loan document states what must happen when a loan must be paid immediately; but usually it applies to nonpayment, late payments, or the transfer of the property without the lender's permission.

Adjustable-Rate Mortgage (ARM) A loan program where the interest rate may change throughout the life of the loan. An ARM adjusts based on terms agreed to between the lender and the borrower, but typically it may only change once or twice a year.

Aggregator Sites Websites that list the rates of many mortgage companies.

Alternate Credit Items you must pay each month but that won't appear on your credit report, such as your telephone bill. In relation to mortgage loans, although such items aren't reported as installment or revolving credit, they can establish your ability and willingness to make consistent payments in a responsible manner. Sometimes called *nonstandard credit*.

Alt Loans Alternative loans, so-called because they're not conventional or government loans but step outside the lending box and establish their own lending criteria.

Amortization Amortization is the length of time it takes for a loan to be fully paid off, by predetermined agreement. These payments are at regular intervals. Sometimes called a *fully amortized* loan. Amortization terms can vary, but generally accepted terms run in 5-year increments, from 10 to 40 years.

Annual Percentage Rate (APR) The cost of money borrowed, expressed as an annual rate. The APR is a useful consumer tool to compare different lenders, but unfortunately it is often not used correctly. The APR can work only when comparing the same exact loan type from one lender to another.

Appraisable Asset Any item whose value can be determined by a third-party expert. That car you want to sell is an appraisable asset. If the item can be appraised, then you can use those funds to buy a house.

Appraisal A report that helps to determine the market value of a property. An appraisal can be done in various ways, as required by a lender, from simply driving by the property to ordering a full-blown inspection, complete with full-color photographs. Appraisals compare similar homes in the area to substantiate the value of the property in question.

APR *See* Annual Percentage Rate.

ARM *See* Adjustable-Rate Mortgage.

Assumable Mortgage Homes sold with assumable mortgages let buyers take over the terms of the loan along with the house being sold. Assumable loans may be fully or non-qualifying assumable, meaning buyers take over the loan without being qualified or otherwise evaluated by the original lender. Qualifying assumable loans mean that although buyers may assume terms of the existing note, they must qualify all over again as if they were applying for a brand-new loan.

AUS *See* Automated Underwriting System.

Automated Underwriting System (AUS) A software application that electronically issues a preliminary loan approval. An AUS uses a complex approval matrix that reviews credit reports, debt ratios, and other factors that go into a mortgage loan approval.

Automated Valuation Model (AVM) An electronic method of evaluating a property's appraised value, done by scanning public records for recent home sales and other data in the subject property's neighborhood. Although not yet widely accepted as a replacement for full-blown appraisals, many in the industry expect AVMs to eventually replace traditional appraisals altogether.

AVM *See* Automated Valuation Model.

Balloon Mortgage A type of mortgage where the remaining balance must be paid in full at the end of a preset term. A 5-year balloon mortgage might be amortized over a 30-year period, but the remaining balance is due, in full, at the end of 5 years.

Basis Point A basis point is $1/100$ percent change in rate. A move of 50 basis points would cause a 30-year fixed mortgage rate to change by $1/8$ percent.

Bridge Loan A short-term loan primarily used to pull equity out of one property for a down payment on another. This loan is paid off when the original property sells. Because they are short-term loans, sometimes lasting just a few weeks, customarily only retail banks offer them. Usually the borrower doesn't make any monthly payments and pays off the loan only when the property sells.

Bundling Bundling is the act of putting together several real estate or mortgage services in one package. Instead of paying for an appraisal here or an inspection there, some or all of the buyer's services are packaged together. Usually a bundle offers discounts on all services, although when they're bundled it's hard to parse all the services to see whether you're getting a good deal.

Buydown Paying more money to get a lower interest rates is called a *permanent* buydown, and it is used in conjunction with discount points. The more points, the lower the rate. A *temporary* buydown is a fixed rate mortgage that starts at a reduced rate for the first period and then gradually increases to its final note rate. A temporary buydown for two years is called a 2-1 buydown. For three years it's called a 3-2-1 buydown.

Cash-Out A refinance mortgage that involves taking equity out of a home in the form of cash during a refinance. Instead of just reducing your interest rate during a refinance and financing your closing costs, you finance even more, putting the additional money in your pocket.

Closer The person who helps prepare the lender's closing documents. The closer forwards those documents to your settlement agent's office, where you will be signing closing papers. In other states, a closer can be the person who holds your loan closing.

Closing Costs The various fees involved when buying a home or obtaining a mortgage. The fees, required to issue a good loan, can come directly from the lender or may come from others in the transactions.

Collateral Collateral is property owned by the borrower that's pledged to the lender as security in case the loan goes bad.

A lender makes a mortgage with the house as collateral.

Comparable Sales Comparable sales are that part of an appraisal report that lists recent transfers of similar properties in the immediate vicinity of the property being bought. Also called "comps."

Conforming Loan A conventional conforming loan is a Fannie Mae or Freddie Mac loan that is equal to or less than the maximum allowable loan limits established by Fannie and Freddie. These limits are changed annually.

Conventional Loan A loan mortgage that uses guidelines established by Fannie Mae or Freddie Mac and is issued and guaranteed by lenders.

Correspondent Banker (also Correspondent Lender) A mortgage banker that doesn't intend to keep your mortgage loan but instead sells your loan to another preselected mortgage banker. Correspondent bankers are smaller mortgage bankers, those perhaps with a regional presence but not a national one.

They can shop various rates from other correspondent mortgage bankers that have set up an established relationship to buy and sell loans from one another. They operate much like a broker, except correspondent bankers use their own money to fund loans.

Credit Report A report that shows the payment histories of a consumer, along with the individual's property addresses and any public records.

Credit Repository A place where credit histories are stored. Merchants and banks agree to store consumers' credit patterns in a central place that other merchants and banks can access.

Credit Score A number derived from a consumer's credit history and based upon various credit details in a consumer's past and upon the likelihood of default. Different credit patterns are assigned different numbers, and different credit activity may have a greater or lesser impact on the score. The higher the credit score, the better the credit.

Debt Consolidation Paying off all or part of one's consumer debt with equity from a home. Debit consolidation can be part of a refinanced mortgage or a separate equity loan.

Debt Ratio Gross monthly payments divided by gross monthly income, expressed as a percentage. There are typically two debt ratios to be considered: The *housing ratio*—sometimes called the *front-end* or *front ratio*—is the total monthly house payment, plus any monthly tax, insurance, private mortgage insurance, or HOA dues, divided by gross monthly income. The *total debt ratio*—also called the *back-end* or *back ratio*—is the total housing payment plus other monthly consumer installment or revolving debt, also expressed as a percentage. Loan debt ratio guidelines are usually denoted as 32/38, with 32 being the front ratio and the 38 being the back ratio. Ratio guidelines can vary from loan to loan and lender to lender.

Deed A written document evidencing each transfer of ownership in a property.

Deed of Trust A written document giving an interest in the
home being bought to a third party, usually the lender, as
security to the lender.

Delinquent Being behind on a mortgage payment.
Delinquencies typically are recognized as 30+ days' delinquent, 60+ days' delinquent, and 90+ days' delinquent.

Discount Points Also called "points," they are represented as a
percentage of a loan amount. One point equals 1 percent of
a loan balance. Borrowers pay discount points to reduce
the interest rate for a mortgage. Typically each discount
point paid reduces the interest rate by $1/4$ percent. It is a
form of prepaid interest to a lender.

Disposable Income Disposable income is the amount of money
left over every month to goof around with—go to the
movies, fill up the car with gas, or invest in a retirement
fund.

Document Stamp Evidence—usually with an ink stamp—of
how much tax was paid upon transfer of ownership of
property. Certain states call it a *doc stamp*. Doc stamp tax
rates can vary based upon locale, and not all states have doc
stamps.

Down Payment The amount of money initially given by the
borrower to close a mortgage. The down payment equals

the sales price less financing. It's the very first bit of equity you'll have in the new home.

Easement A right of way previously established by a third party. Easement types can vary but typically involve the right of a public utility to cross your land to access an electrical line.

Entitlement The amount the VA will guarantee for a VA loan to be made. *See also* VA Loan.

Equity The difference between the appraised value of a home and any outstanding loans recorded against the house.

Escrow Depending upon where you live, escrow can mean two things. On the West Coast, for example, when a home goes under contract it "goes into escrow" (*see also* Escrow Agent). In other parts of the country, an escrow is a financial account set up by a lender to collect monthly installments for annual tax bills and/or hazard insurance policy renewals.

Escrow Account *See* Impound Account.

Escrow Agent On the West Coast, the escrow agent is the person or company that handles the home closing, ensuring documents are assigned correctly and property transfer has legitimately changed hands.

FACTA *See* Fair and Accurate Credit Transactions Act.

Fair and Accurate Credit Transactions Act (FACTA) The FACTA is a new law that replaces the Fair Credit Reporting Act, or

FCRA, and governs how consumer information can be stored, shared, and monitored for privacy and accuracy.

Fair Credit Reporting Act (FCRA) The FCRA was the first consumer law that emphasized rights and protections relating to consumers' credit reports, their credit applications, and privacy concerns.

Fannie Mae See Federal National Mortgage Association.

Farmers Home Administration (FmHA) The FmHA provides financing to farmers and other qualified borrowers who are unable to obtain loans elsewhere. These loans are typical for rural properties that might be larger in acreage than a suburban home, as well as for working farms.

FCRA See Fair Credit Reporting Act.

Fed Shorthand for the Federal Reserve Board.

Federal Home Loan Mortgage Corporation (FHLMC) The FHLMC, or Freddie Mac, is a corporation established by the U.S. government in 1968 to buy mortgages from lenders made under Freddie Mac guidelines.

Federal Housing Administration (FHA) The FHA was formed in 1934 and is now a division of the Department of Housing and Urban Development (HUD). It provides loan guarantees to lenders who make loans under FHA guidelines.

Federal National Mortgage Association (FNMA) The FNMA, or Fannie Mae, was originally established in 1938 by the U.S.

government to buy FHA mortgages and provide liquidity in the mortgage marketplace. It is similar in function to Freddie Mac. In 1968, its charter was changed and it now purchases conventional mortgages as well as government ones.

Federal Reserve Board The head of the Federal Reverse Banks that, among other things, sets overnight lending rates for banking institutions. The Fed does not set mortgage rates.

Fed Funds Rate The rate banks charge one another to borrow money overnight.

Fee Income The closing costs received by a lender or broker that is outside the interest rate or discount points. Fee income can be in the form of loan-processing charges, underwriting fees, and the like.

FHA *See* Federal Housing Administration.

FICO FICO stands for Fair Isaac Corporation, the company that invented the most widely used credit scoring system.

Final Inspection The last inspection of a property, showing that a new home being built is 100 percent complete or that home improvement is 100 percent complete. It lets lenders know that their collateral and their loan are exactly where they should be.

Financed Premium An alternative to second mortgages and mortgage insurance that allows the borrower to buy a mortgage insurance premium and roll the cost of the premium into the loan amount, in lieu of paying a mortgage insurance payment every month.

Fixed-Rate Mortgage A loan whose interest rate does not change throughout the term of the loan.

Float Actively deciding not to "lock" or guarantee an interest rate while a loan is being processed. A float is usually done because the borrower believes rates will go down.

Float-Down A mortgage loan rate that can drop as mortgage rates drop. Usually a loan comes in two types of float, one being during construction of a home and the other being during the period of an interest rate lock.

Flood Certificate A certificate that shows whether a property or part of a property lies above or below any local flood zones. These flood zones are mapped over the course of several years by the Federal Emergency Management Agency (FEMA). The certificate identifies the property's exact legal location and a flood line's elevation. There is a box that simply asks, "Is the property in a flood zone, yes or no?" If the property is in a flood zone, the lender will require special flood insurance that is not usually carried under a standard homeowners hazard insurance policy.

FmHA See Farmers Home Administration.

Foreclosure A foreclosure is the bad thing that happens when the mortgage isn't repaid. Lenders begin the process of forcefully recovering their collateral when borrowers fail to make loan payments. The lender takes your house away.

Freddie Mac See Federal Home Loan Mortgage Corporation.

Fully Indexed Rate The number reached when adding a loan's index and the margin. This rate is how adjustable note rates are compiled.

Funding The actual transfer of money from a lender to a borrower.

Funding Fee A required fee, equal to 2 percent of the sales price of a home, that helps to fund a VA loan guarantee.

Gift When the down payment and closing costs for a home are given to the borrower instead of the funds coming from their own accounts, it is called a gift. Usually such gifts can come only from family members or foundations established to help new homeowners.

Gift Affidavit A form signed whereby someone swears that the money she is giving you is indeed a gift, not a loan, and is to be used for the purchase of a home. Lenders like to see that form, as well as a paper trail of the gift funds being added to your own funds.

Gift Funds Monies given to a borrower for the sole purpose of buying a home. These funds are not to be paid back in any form and are usually given by a family member or a qualified nonprofit organization.

Ginnie Mae See Government National Mortgage Association.

Good-Faith Estimate A list of estimated closing costs on a particular mortgage transaction. This estimate must be provided to the loan applicants within 72 hours after receipt of a mortgage application by the lender or broker.

Government National Mortgage Association (GNMA) The GNMA, or Ginnie Mae, is a U.S. government corporation formed to purchase government loans like VA and FHA loans from banks and mortgage lenders. Think of it as Fannie or Freddie, only it buys government loans.

Hazard Insurance A specific type of insurance that covers against certain destructive elements such as fire, wind, and hail. It is usually an addition to homeowners insurance, but every home loan has a hazard rider.

HELOC *See* Home Equity Line of Credit.

Hold-Back A contingency fund associated with a construction or re-model. It covers any change orders that might occur during the process. A *change order* is what happens when you simply change your mind. The hold-back helps pay for the change when changing your mind costs more than the loan. A typical hold-back amount is 10 percent of the original loan.

Home Equity Line of Credit (HELOC) HELOC is a credit line using a home as collateral. Customers write checks on this line of credit whenever they need to and pay only on balances withdrawn. It is much like a credit card but secured by the property.

Homeowners Insurance An insurance policy that covers not just hazard items, but also other things, such as liability or personal property.

Hybrid Loan A cross between an ARM and a fixed-rate loan. In a hybrid loan, the rate is fixed for a predetermined number of years before turning into an adjustable-rate mortgage, or ARM.

Impound Account An account that is set up by a lender to deposit a monthly portion of annual property taxes or hazard insurance. As taxes or insurance come up for renewal, the lender pays the bill using these funds. Also called an *escrow account.*

Index An index is used as the basis to establish an interest rate, usually associated with a margin. Almost anything can be an index, but the most common are U.S. Treasuries or similar instruments. *See also* Fully Indexed Rate.

Inspection A structural review of the house to determine defects in workmanship, damage to the property, or required maintenance. An inspection does not determine the value of the property. A pest inspection, for example, looks for termites or wood ants.

Installment Account Borrowing one lump sum and agreeing to pay back a certain amount each month until the loan is paid off. A car loan is an example of an installment loan.

Intangible Asset An asset not by itself, but by what it represents. A publicly traded stock is an intangible asset. It's not the stock itself that has the value, but what the stock represents in terms of income.

Intangible Tax A state tax on personal property.

Interest-Only Loan A loan that requires only that you pay the interest on your loan each month, without having to pay any part of the principal.

Interest Rate The amount charged to borrowed money over a specified period of time.

Interest Rate Reduction Loan (IRRL) An IRRL is a VA refinance loan program that has relaxed credit guidelines. Also called a *streamline refinance*.

IRRL *See* Interest Rate Reduction Loan.

Jumbo Loan A mortgage that exceeds current conforming loan limits. For 2007, anything above $417,000 was considered jumbo.

Junior Lien A second mortgage or one that subordinates to another loan. Not as common a term as it used to be. You're more likely to hear the terms *second mortgage* or *piggyback*.

Land Contract An arrangement where the buyer makes monthly payments to the seller but the ownership of the property does not change hands until the loan is paid in full.

Land-to-Value An appraisal term that calculates the value of the land as a percentage of the total value of the home. If the land exceeds the value of the home, it's more difficult to find financing without good comparable sales. Also called *lot-to-value*.

Lease-Purchase Agreement Also known as *rent-to-own*. An option whereby a buyer leases a home until the buyer has saved up enough money for down payment to qualify for a conventional mortgage.

Lender Policy Title insurance that protects a mortgage from defects or previous claims of ownership.

Liability An obligation or bill on the part of the borrower. It works like an automobile loan. When you pay off the car, you get the title. Liabilities such as student loans or a car payments can show up on a credit report, but they can also be anything else that you are obligated to pay. Those liabilities on the credit report are used to determine debt ratios.

LIBOR Index *See* London Interbank Offered Rate.

Lien A legal claim or prior interest on the property you're about to buy. Borrowing money from another source to buy a house could mean that someone else has a lien on that property.

Loan Money granted to one party with the expectation of it being repaid.

Loan Officer The person typically responsible for helping mortgage applicants get qualified and assisting in loan selection and loan application. Loan officers can work at banks, credit unions, or mortgage brokerage houses or for bankers.

Loan Processor The person who gathers the required documentation for a loan application for loan submission. Along with your loan officer, you'll work with the loan processor quite a bit during your mortgage process.

Loan-to-Value Ratio (LTV) LTV is expressed as a percentage of the loan amount when compared to the valuation of the home determined by an appraisal. If a home was appraised at $100,000 and the loan amount was $70,000, then the LTV would be 70 percent.

Loan Underwriter The person responsible for ultimately saying "yes" or "no" on a loan file. The underwriter compares loan guidelines with what you have documented in the file.

Lock An agreement guaranteeing an interest rate over a predetermined period of time. Loan locks are not loan approvals; they're simply the rate your lender has agreed to give you at the loan closing.

London Interbank Offered Rate (LIBOR) LIBOR is a British index similar to our federal funds rate, where British banks borrow money from one another over short periods to adhere to reserve requirements.

LTV *See* Loan-to-Value Ratio.

Margin A number, expressed as a percentage, that is added to a mortgage's index to determine the rate the borrower pays on the note. An index can be a six-month CD at 4 percent and the margin can be 2 percent. The interest rate the borrower pays is 4 + 2, or 6 percent. A *fully indexed rate* is the index plus the margin.

Market Gain The difference between what a mortgage price was when you locked it with the lender and what the mortgage price is when the loan is physically locked with the lender's secondary department or with a mortgage broker's wholesale lender.

Market Value In an open market, the market value of a property is both the most the borrower is willing to pay and the least the seller is willing to accept at the time of contract. Property appraisals help justify market value by comparing similar home sales in the subject property's neighborhood.

Modifiable Mortgage A mortgage loan that allows its interest rate to be modified, even if it's at another lender.

Mortgage A loan with the property being pledged as collateral. The mortgage is retired when the loan is paid in full.

Mortgage-Backed Securities Investment securities issued by Wall Street firms that are guaranteed, or collateralized, with home mortgages taken out by consumers. These securities can then be bought and sold on Wall Street.

Mortgage Bankers Lenders who use their own funds to lend

money. Historically, these funds would have come from the savings accounts of other bank customers. But with the evolution of mortgage banking, that's the old way of doing business. Even though bankers use their own money, it may come from other sources such as lines of credit or through selling loans to other institutions.

Mortgage Brokers Companies that set up a home loan between a banker and a borrower. Brokers don't have money to lend directly, but they have experience in finding various loan programs that can suit the borrower, similar to how an independent insurance agent operates. Brokers don't work for the borrower but instead provide mortgage loan choices from other mortgage lenders.

Mortgagee The person or business making the loan; also called the *lender*.

Mortgage Insurance (MI) *See* Private Mortgage Insurance.

Mortgagor The person(s) getting the loan; also called the *borrower*.

Multiple-Listing Service (MLS) MLS is a central repository where real estate brokers and agents show homes and search for homes that are for sale.

Negative Amortization A neg-am loan is an adjustable-rate mortgage that can have two interest rates, the *contract rate* or the *fully indexed rate*. The contract rate is the minimum agreed-upon rate the consumer must pay; sometimes the contract rate is lower than the fully indexed rate. The borrower has a choice of which rate to pay, but if the contract rate is lower than the fully indexed rate, that difference is added back to the loan. If your contract payments are only $500 but the fully indexed rate is $700 and you pay only the contract rate, $200 is added back into your original loan amount. Not for the fainthearted, nor for those with little money down.

NINA No Income, No Asset Mortgage. This type of loan does not require that the borrower prove or otherwise document any income or asset whatsoever.

No-Fee Loan A loan where your lender pays closing costs for you, if you agree to a slightly higher interest rate.

Nonconforming Loans whose amounts are above current Fannie or Freddie limits. *See also* Jumbo Loan.

Note A promise to repay. It may or may not have property involved and may or may not be a mortgage.

Note Modification Taking the original terms of a note, and without changing any other part of the obligation or title, reducing the interest rate for the remaining term of the loan. A note modification means you can't "shop around" for the best rate to reduce your rate; instead, you must work with your original lender who still services your mortgage. In a modification, nothing can change except the rate.

One-Time Close Loan A construction loan whereby you obtain construction financing and permanent financing and lock in a permanent mortgage rate at the same time. *See also* Two-Time Close Loan.

Origination Fee A fee charged to cover costs associated with finding, documenting, and preparing a mortgage application, and usually expressed as a percentage of the loan amount.

Owner's Policy Title insurance made for the benefit of the homeowner.

Par An interest rate that can be obtained without paying any discount points and that does not have any additional yield beyond its rate. For instance, you get a 30-year quote of 7.00 percent with one point, or 7.25 percent with zero points, or 7.50 percent with zero points plus an additional yield to you of $1,000 toward closing costs. Here, the 7.25 percent at zero points is the par rate.

Payment-Option ARM A type of negative amortization loan where you have a choice as to what you'd like to pay each month. The choice is between an initial contract rate, an interest interest-only, or a fully indexed, fully amortized loan.

Payment Shock A term used by lenders referring to the percentage difference between what you're paying now for housing and what your new payment would be. Most loan programs don't have a payment shock provision, but for those that do, a common percentage increase is 150 percent.

Permanent Buydown See Buydown.

Piggyback Mortgage See Second Mortgage.

PITI Principal, Interest, Taxes, and Insurance. These figures are used to help determine front-debt ratios. In condos, townhouses, or co-ops, HOA dues replace the payment for insurance.

Pledged Asset An appraisable property or security that is collateralized to make a mortgage loan. Sometimes a pledged asset can be a stock or mutual fund. A lender can make a mortgage loan and use the mutual fund as part of the collateral. If the borrower fails to make the payments, all or part of the pledged asset can go to the lender.

PMI See Private Mortgage Insurance.

Points See Discount Points.

Portfolio Loan A loan made by a direct lender, usually a bank, and kept in the lender's loan portfolio instead of being sold or underwritten to any external guidelines.

Predatory Loan A loan designed to take advantage of people by charging either too many fees or too high an interest rate, or both, while also stripping those homeowners of their equity.

Prepaid Interest Daily interest collected from the day of loan closing to the first of the following month.

Prepayment Penalty An amount is paid to the lender if the loan is paid off before its maturity or if extra payments are made on the loan. A *hard penalty* is automatic if the loan is paid off early or if extra payments are made at any time or for any amount whatsoever. A *soft penalty* only lasts for a couple of years and may allow extra payments on the loan, not to exceed a certain amount.

Principal The outstanding amount owed on a loan, not including any interest due.

Private Mortgage Insurance (PMI) PMI is typically required on all mortgage loans with less than 20 percent down. It is an insurance policy, paid by the borrower, with benefits paid to the lender. It covers the difference between the borrower's down payment and 20 percent of the sales price. If the borrower defaults on the mortgage, this difference is paid to the lender.

Pull-Through Rate A term, used by wholesale lenders, to track the percentage of loans that close that have been locked by a broker.

Quit Claim A release of any interest in a property from one party to another. A quit claim does not, however, release the obligation on the mortgage.

Rate-and-Term Refinance Refinancing to get a new rate. You're changing the interest rate and changing the term, or length, of the new note.

Rate Cap How high your ARM rate is permitted to change each adjustment period. There are three possible caps on an adjustable-rate mortgage: the adjustment cap, the lifetime rate cap, and the initial rate cap.

Real Estate Account A mortgage secured by real estate.

Realtor A member of the National Association of REALTORS and a registered trademark. Not all real estate agents are Realtors.

Recast A term applied to ARMs and used when extra payments are made to the principal balance. When your note is recast, your monthly payment is calculated for you.

Refinance Obtaining a new mortgage to replace an existing one. *See also* Rate-and-Term Refinance, where only the outstanding principal balance, interest due, and closing costs are included in the loan.

Reissue When refinancing, there may be discounts if you use the same title agency. This "reissue" of an original title report can cost much less than a full title insurance policy.

Rescission Withdrawal from a mortgage agreement. Refinanced mortgage loans for a primary residence have a required three-day "cooling off" period before the loan becomes official. If for any reason you decide not to take the mortgage, you can "rescind" and the whole deal's off.

Reserves A borrower's assets after closing. Reserves can include cash in the bank, stocks, mutual funds, retirement accounts, IRAs, and 401(k) accounts.

Reverse Mortgage A mortgage designed to help older

Americans who own their homes by paying the homeowners cash in exchange for the equity in their home. When the homeowners no longer own the home by selling or moving out or dying, then the reverse mortgage lender is paid back all the money borrowed, plus interest.

Revolving Account A credit card or department store account on which you typically have a limit and don't make any payments until you charge something.

Sales Contract Your written agreement to sell or purchase a home, signed by both the seller and buyer.

Secondary Market A financial arena where mortgages are bought and sold, either individually or grouped together into securities backed by those mortgages. Fannie Mae and Freddie Mac are the backbone for the conventional secondary market. Other secondary markets exist for nonconforming loans, subprime loans, and others.

Second Mortgage Sometimes called a "piggyback" mortgage, a second mortgage assumes a subordinate position behind a first mortgage. If the home goes into foreclosure, the first mortgage would be settled before the second could lay claim. *See also* Junior Lien.

Seller The person transferring ownership and all rights for your home in exchange for cash or trade.

Settlement Statement Also called the Final HUD-1. It shows all financial entries during the home sale, including sales price, closing costs, loan amounts, and property taxes. Your initial good-faith estimate will be your first glimpse of your settlement statement. This statement is one of the final documents put together before you go to closing and is prepared by your attorney or settlement agent.

Subprime Loan A loan made to people with less than "prime" credit. There are various stages of subprime credit, from loans for those with simply "tarnished" credit who can't quite get a conventional mortgage to those with seriously damaged credit who may be in or just out of bankruptcy or have collection accounts or judgments and liens against them.

Survey A map that shows the physical location of the structure and where it sits on the property. A survey also designates any easements that run across or through the property.

Temporary Buydown *See* Buydown.

Title Legal ownership in a property.

Title Exam/Title Search The process where public records are reviewed to research any previous liens on the property.

Title Insurance Protection for the lender, the seller, and/or the borrower against any defects or previous claims to the property being transferred or sold.

Two-Time Close Loan In a construction financing, when you first get a construction loan and then get another mortgage at the end of construction. You'll go to two different closings for a two-time close loan. *See also* One-Time Close Loan.

VA Loan Government mortgage guaranteed by the Department of Veterans Affairs.

VA No-No A type of VA loan where the borrower not only puts *no* money down but also pays *no* closing costs.

Verification of Deposit (VOD) A VOD is a form mailed to a bank or credit union that asks the institution to verify that a borrower's bank account exists, how much is in it, how long the borrower has had it, and what the average balance was over the previous two months.

VOD *See* Verification of Deposit.

Wraparound Mortgage A method of financing where the borrower pays the former owner of the property each month in the form of a mortgage payment. The former owner will then make a mortgage payment to the original mortgage holder.

| I N D E X |

Look for These Informative Real Estate Titles at www.amacombooks.org/go/realestate

A Survival Guide for Buying a Home, Second Edition
by Sid Davis $17.95

A Survival Guide for Selling a Home by Sid Davis $15.00

An Insider's Guide to Refinancing Your Mortgage
by David Reed $16.95

Are You Dumb Enough to Be Rich?, Second Edition
by G. William Barnett II $18.95

Everything You Need to Know Before Buying a Co-op, Condo, or Townhouse by Ken Roth $18.95

Financing Your Condo, Co-op, or Townhouse by David Reed $18.95

Mortgages 101, Second Edition by David Reed $16.95

Mortgage Confidential by David Reed $16.95

Real Estate Investing Made Simple by M. Anthony Carr $17.95

Stop Foreclosure Now by Lloyd Segal $19.95

The Complete Guide to Investing in Foreclosures
by Steve Berges $17.95

The First-Time Homeowner's Survival Guide by Sid Davis $16.00

The Home Buyer's Question and Answer Book
by Bridget McCrea $16.95

The Landlord's Financial Tool Kit by Michael C. Thomsett $18.95

The Property Management Tool Kit by Mike Beirne $19.95

The Real Estate Investor's Pocket Calculator
by Michael C. Thomsett $17.95

The Successful Landlord by Ken Roth $19.95

Who Says You Can't Buy a Home! by David Reed $17.95

Your Eco-Friendly Home by Sid Davis $17.95

Your Guide to VA Loans by David Reed $17.95